String Quilts with Style

String Quilts with Style

Bobbie Aug & Sharon Newman

American Quilter's Society
P. O. Box 3290 • Paducah, KY 42002-3290

Located in Paducah, Kentucky, the American Quilter's Society (AQS) is dedicated to promoting the accomplishments of today's quilters. Through its publications and events, AQS strives to honor today's quiltmakers and their work and to inspire future creativity and innovation in quiltmaking.

EDITOR: BARBARA SMITH
ASSISTANT EDITOR: ELEANOR LEVIE
BOOK DESIGN/ILLUSTRATIONS: ELAINE WILSON
COVER DESIGN: MICHAEL BUCKINGHAM
PHOTOGRAPHY: CHARLES R. LYNCH

Library of Congress Cataloging-in-Publication Data

Aug, Bobbie A.
      String quilts with style / Bobbie Aug & Sharon Newman.
      p.   cm.
      ISBN 1-57432-720-8
      1. Patchwork--Patterns.   2. Quilting Patterns.   I. Newman, Sharon,
1942–   .   II. Title.
TT835.A88   1999
746.46'041--dc21   99-14407
                                                                CIP

Additional copies of this book may be ordered from the American Quilter's Society, PO Box 3290, Paducah, KY 42002-3290 @ $18.95. Add $2.00 for postage and handling.

Printed in the U.S.A. by Image Graphics, Paducah, KY

CONTENTS

ACKNOWLEDGMENTS

We are truly grateful to Meredith Schroeder, president of the American Quilter's Society, for giving us an opportunity to spend many enjoyable hours together compiling this book. It was great fun! Also, we wish to thank our husbands, Norm Aug and Tom Newman, for supporting us in this effort.

1898 STARS IN GARDEN MAZE, 95" x 95", by SHARON NEWMAN. Stars pieced on 1898 newspaper were joined with vintage fabrics in this classic setting.

GREEN SPIDERWEB, 67" x 84", by HULDA NIEMAN. Made in the late 1930s by Hulda Nieman and given to her daughter, Ester Klaus, in Wilson, Texas.

INTRODUCTION

The purpose of this book is to introduce you to structured string piecing – an easy-to-do method of making scrap quilts. We have created exciting and graphic quilts incorporating a variety of settings and patterns, color organization, and contrasting backgrounds. These quilts showcase the beauty of contemporary fabrics while maintaining a tie with tradition.

In the past, utilitarian string-pieced quilts were made of the last scraps from home-sewn dresses, shirts, aprons, and home furnishings. Thrifty quiltmakers used these little pieces of fabric by cutting them into short, narrow strips. The strips were then sewn to paper or cloth foundations to ensure that the little pieces would have stability for use in a quilt pattern.

Whatever cloth was most available was used for fabric foundations, and quilts sewn in this way may exhibit a patchwork of different foundation prints, continuing the use-every-bit economy. Foundations were sometimes cut from newspapers, catalogs, or magazine pages instead of cloth. The news thereby preserved is interesting. Stories of the farm economy and stories from the West were used for the diamonds in an 1898 eight-pointed star. One set of pieces, done on catalog pages from 1928, makes a person long for 13-cents-per-yard, high-grade muslin and 17-cents-per-yard dress goods. The newspapers are usually a good indicator of the time a work was sewn, because few people kept newspapers for very long before using them for foundation piecing.

The sewing machine was often used to sew the strings to a foundation, but some quiltmakers stitched the pieces on papers by hand. A few pieces of cloth and a couple of paper shapes made good take-along sewing.

Sewing fabric pieces on paper squares, diamonds, triangles, and other shapes was often the way a young person learned to use a sewing machine. Elderly or invalid ladies often hand sewed pieces cut by daughters who were caring for them and who wanted their mothers to feel productive.

A few pieces of cloth and a couple of paper shapes made good take-along sewing.

We hope
you
will enjoy
this
method of
quilt-
making
as much as
we have.

Today, quiltmakers have rediscovered the advantages of sewing on foundations. As we explore the history of quiltmaking and adapt the styles and patterns to our present day, the string-pieced quilt has been transformed from a way to use "everything left over" to a means of creating a scrap quilt with structure and style.

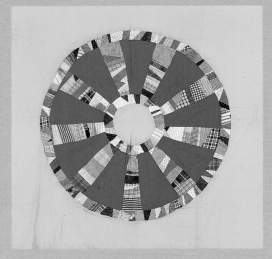

SUNDIAL, detail of front.

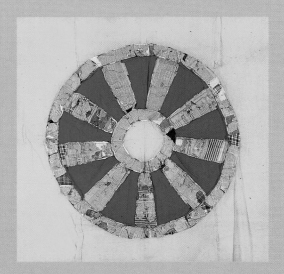

SUNDIAL, detail of back. Notice the papers still in place in this unusual turn-of-the-century piece.

SECTION

ONE

BASIC STRING PIECING

BASIC STRING PIECING

As the term is used here, a "string" is a long narrow strip of fabric. Strings can be any length and can vary in width. In this book, they range from ½" to 4" wide, but most average about 1" – 1½" wide. The strings need not be even or symmetrical, since the beauty of the technique is in the asymmetrical appearance.

Strings are sewn to a paper or fabric foundation to provide a temporary base for the pattern pieces. Paper foundations are removed before the quilt is layered with batting and backing. Fabric foundations are left in place, making the finished piece heavier and more difficult to hand quilt. Therefore, fabric-foundation quilts can be machine quilted or tied. We have chosen to use paper foundations for all the quilts in this book.

STRING-PIECING SUPPLIES

FOUNDATION PAPER. Any thin, lightweight paper will do. Tissue paper and parchment paper are good choices and are easy to remove. Other possibilities include tracing paper, freezer paper, or thin typing paper. As vintage quilts show us, newsprint is also a possibility, though newspaper ink will soil the fabrics. Rolls of unprinted newsprint can usually be purchased where newspapers are published.

PINS. We prefer fine pins for minimal distortion.

SCISSORS. Keep a pair right at the sewing machine for trimming strings and threads. You can cut the foundation papers with paper-cutting scissors or with your rotary cutter outfitted with an old blade. Fabrics can be cut with fabric scissors or rotary cutter.

RULERS. These are needed for drafting foundation shapes and for use with a rotary cutter. The 6" x 24" rotary ruler is a basic tool, and the 6" or 8" square rulers are convenient.

CLEAR PLASTIC ACETATE. Use acetate to make templates for marking patches, sashing squares, and short sashing strips. Templates can be plain or marked with a grid.

SEWING MACHINE. Strings can be sewn to a foundation with a sewing machine. You may want to fill several bobbins because this process uses quite a bit of thread. Choose a good-quality thread, as you would for any other quiltmaking. Use a size 12 machine needle and shorten your stitches to 12 – 15 per inch. The quilts in this book were all assembled by machine, and many of them were quilted by machine as well.

MAKING TEMPLATES

Some patches in the quilts may require making templates. For convenience, use clear plastic acetate to make them. The type of acetate marked with a grid makes it easy to cut true 90° angles and to line up the grain of the fabrics you will be cutting. Cut templates for machine stitching with the ¼" seam allowance included. With a fine, permanent marker, carefully trace each different shape to be used in a pattern on template material and cut out carefully along the marked lines. When tracing patterns for templates, be sure to include the arrows for aligning the patterns with the fabric grain. Use templates to mark fabric on the wrong side, keeping a sharp pencil or chalk point as close to the template edges as possible. A 0.5mm mechanical pencil is useful for marking all but the darkest of fabrics, for which you can use a white pencil. Cut the fabric along the marked lines.

A "STRING" IS A LONG, NARROW STRIP OF FABRIC.

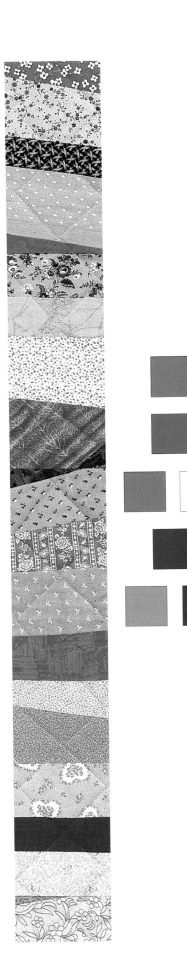

PLANNING FABRICS AND COLORS

Choose 100% cotton scraps for ease in sewing the string-pieced units. Mix plaids, solids, stripes, and prints. While each set of directions suggests an approximate total amount of fabric for strings, you will need to determine specific amounts for each fabric. Be sure to have enough of any colors that predominate, repeat, or act as an accent. Since you will be making fabric choices as you string-piece, it's a good idea to plan for extra fabric so you can have complete freedom of choice as you work.

Before you begin to sew, sort your fabrics by color. Within each color, divide your scraps into light, medium, and dark. Consider the balance of your fabrics. You may find you need to add a few lights or darks.

Traditional color combinations (such as red and green; pink and blue; red, white, and blue; purple and teal; or tan, rust, and brown) are attractive in string-pieced designs. Choose brights with black, or pastels with white or cream. Look for accent fabrics. Antique scrap quilts often have red accents to unify the many different fabrics. Yellow is another accent color often used in antique scrap quilts.

Viewing actual fabrics alongside each other is the best way to reach a satisfying combination for your quilt. However, if the color photograph of the quilt you want to make limits your imagination, you can photocopy the assembly diagram on a black and white copier and use markers or colored pencils to audition other possibilities. It is often helpful to work in stages as follows: Choose fabrics just for the string pieces, and position them in a straight or on-point (diagonal) setting. After you've arranged the string-pieced shapes, audition colors and fabrics for the background patches, the sashing and borders, and even the binding and backing. Cut these pieces out as you are ready for them, rather than all at once in the beginning. Quilters should have the prerogative to change their minds during quilt assembly. Cutting directions for borders and backing provide a bit of extra fabric for adjusting the measurements on these pieces to match the actual finished quilt top.

Prewash all the fabrics you have chosen. Washing them removes the final finishing products and shrinks the fabrics. You can wash in color groups, but watch the process to see if you have dye loss in the first water. For best results, press the fabrics while they are still slightly damp.

STRING-PIECING TECHNIQUE

To begin a string-pieced quilt, decide on the basic shape to be used for the string-pieced portion. Squares, rectangles, triangles, and diamonds – the basic shapes of many patchwork patterns – are popular for string-pieced quilt designs. Cut pieces of paper or fabric in that shape for the foundations. To cut the strings with scissors, you can mark the cutting lines on fabric with a ruler and dressmaker's pencil or chalk. You can also use a rotary cutter to cut strings. For a large quilt, cut long strings across the full width of the fabric. Cut at a slight angle, so that the strings are wider at one end.

Cut a length of string so that it will extend at least ½" beyond the edges of the paper foundation. Place it across the paper near the center (Figure 1–1). Cut and place a second string from a different fabric on the first string, with right sides together and one long edge aligned. Sew the strings together on the aligned edge (Figure 1–2) with a ¼" seam allowance. Lift the top string and press (Figure 1–3). In the same way, sew a string to the opposite side of the center string. Continue adding strings on both sides of the center string, pressing after each addition. Trim the ends of the strings even with the edges of the paper foundation (Figure 1–4).

Piecing can be streamlined with piles of strings and foundations arranged within reach. Just add a string or two to each foundation by chain piecing. Work in convenient-sized batches of string-pieced blocks and press the batch before adding the next set of strings. This type of sewing is good to do with a friend or with a favorite movie on the VCR.

By chain piecing strings, you can reduce the number of steps to the ironing board. Put your ironing board at your elbow to save even more steps. Steam press, making sure the right side is smooth with no little fold at the seam line.

It is important that all seams lie flat and smooth in string-pieced shapes. After each string is sewn, press the seam allowance just sewn to set the seam. Lift up the top strip and press the piece on the right side. Each string should be pressed before another is sewn to it.

Leave paper foundations in place until the quilt top has been completed. This provides stability for the many bias areas and multiple seam lines inherent in the technique and prevents stretching and distortion. The exception to this rule is curved patches, as in Purple Passion, on page 70. In this

STRING PIECING

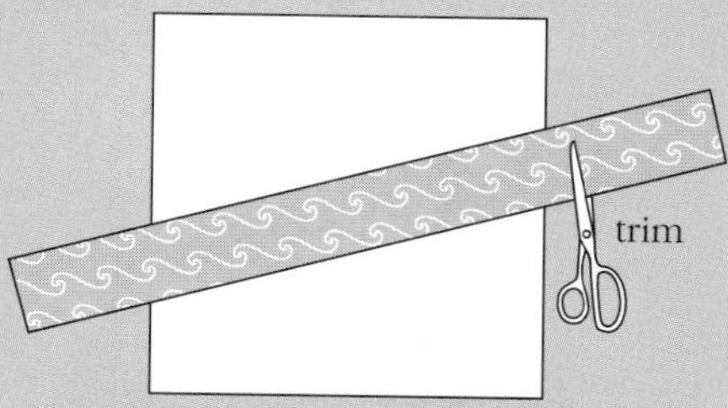

FIGURE 1–1. TRIM STRINGS LARGER THAN FOUNDATION.

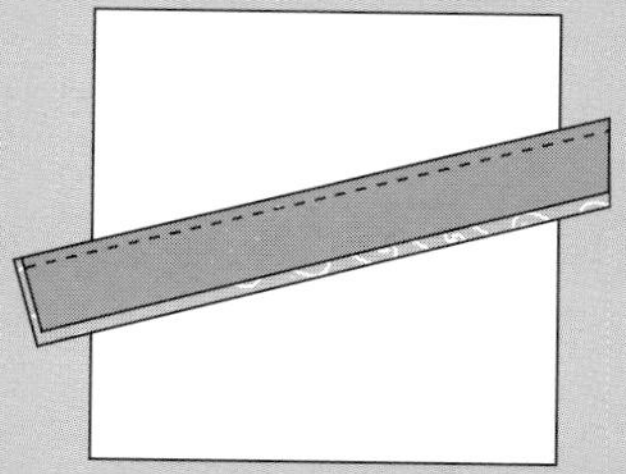

FIGURE 1–2. STITCH NEXT STRING AND PRESS TO SET SEAM.

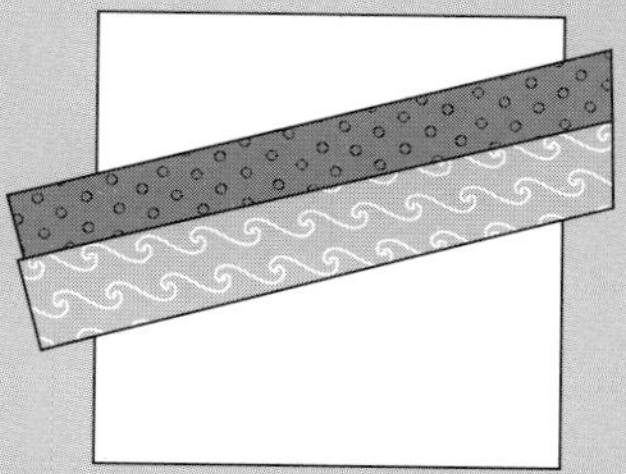

FIGURE 1–3. PRESS STRINGS OPEN.

FIGURE 1–4. TRIM STRINGS EVEN WITH PAPER.

String Piecing a Triangle

pattern, the paper will prevent you from slightly stretching and easing the curves when you join the curved edges.

The small stitches, used to sew the strings, perforate the paper. To remove the foundation, you can use a tool, such as a seam ripper, to score the paper along the seam lines and make an opening in the paper. Pull the paper against the seam lines and it will separate along the stitching. The tool can also help you lift sections of paper easily. Removing the papers is a good activity while traveling or watching a favorite TV program or video.

HOW TO USE THE PATTERNS

Choose a quilt you would like to make. All of these designs adapt beautifully to different color palettes or different sizes. Before you select your fabrics, be sure to read all the directions, especially Basic String Piecing, starting on page 12 and Planning Fabrics and Colors, page 14. Refer to these directions, as needed, as you make your quilt. You will also notice little sign posts labeled "Know-How." These handy references point you to the general directions you may need for making your quilt.

Some of the quilts, such as TAPESTRY and FESTIVAL, are given in two sizes, including a larger version to fit either a double- or queen-size bed. However, any of the quilts can be made smaller or larger. Adjust your fabric needs accordingly. If in doubt, it is better to over estimate the yardage you need to purchase, rather than risk running short.

With each individual quilt project in this book, the finishing details, including the quilting designs, are supplied for your convenience. Feel free to change the patchwork patterns and quilting designs as you like. You can hand or machine quilt your project. If you are new to hand quilting, you may want to refer to a quilting primer or ask a local expert. The same should be said for machine quilting. In either case, it's a good idea to practice on a scrap "sandwich" of fabrics and batting before you work on your quilt.

SECTION

TWO

QUILT
PATTERNS

STRING QUILTS WITH STYLE — BOBBIE AUG & SHARON NEWMAN

TAPESTRY

Quilt size 44" x 62"

Finished string-pieced rectangle 6" x 9"

CUTTING REQUIREMENTS

PAPER FOUNDATIONS
   36 rectangles 6½" x 9½"

SCRAPS 2 yds. equivalent
   Strings average 2½" wide

ACCENT FABRIC 1⅛ yds.
   Center strings average 2½"
      wide
   5 border insert strips 1½"
   wide, cut selvage to selvage

MITERED BORDER 2 yds.
   2 strips 4½" x 64½"
   2 strips 4½" x 46½"

BINDING ¾ yd.
   Cut 2"-wide bias strips from
      24" square

BACKING 4 yds.
   2 panels 24½" x 66"

BATTING 48" x 66"

TAPESTRY, by Bobbie Aug; machine quilted by Janet Spencer.
Rectangles of strings placed on the diagonal are joined in groups
of four to create abstract diamonds. The pink strings laid down the
center of each block give continuity to the design.

TAPESTRY

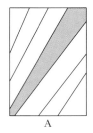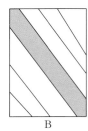

FIGURE 2–1. STRING-PIECED RECTANGLES.

SEWING DIRECTIONS

1 MAKE STRING-PIECED RECTANGLES: Arrange the strings diagonally across each foundation, starting with the accent color in the center. Make 18 A rectangles and 18 B rectangles as shown in Figure 2–1. Trim the strings even with the edges of the paper.

2 ARRANGE RECTANGLES: Arrange the string-pieced rectangles side by side in 6 rows of 6, alternating rectangles A and B to create the design (see Quilt Assembly diagram). Note that the accent strings emphasize the diamond formation created by grouping rectangles.

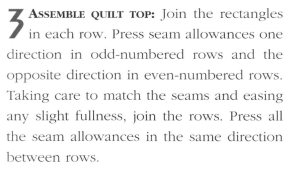

3 ASSEMBLE QUILT TOP: Join the rectangles in each row. Press seam allowances one direction in odd-numbered rows and the opposite direction in even-numbered rows. Taking care to match the seams and easing any slight fullness, join the rows. Press all the seam allowances in the same direction between rows.

4 ADD BORDER INSERT: Measure the length and width of the quilt across the center to determine the exact lengths needed for the border inserts. Sew the 5 border insert strips together to make the lengths needed. Baste the insert strips to the quilt.

5 ATTACH BORDERS: Matching half and quarter measurements, as described for Adding Borders on page 84, pin and sew a 64½" border strip to each side of the quilt and a 46½" strip to the top and bottom. (As you sew, you will catch the border insert in the seams.) Miter the border corners. Press the seam allowances open at the miters and press all others toward the borders. Remove paper foundations.

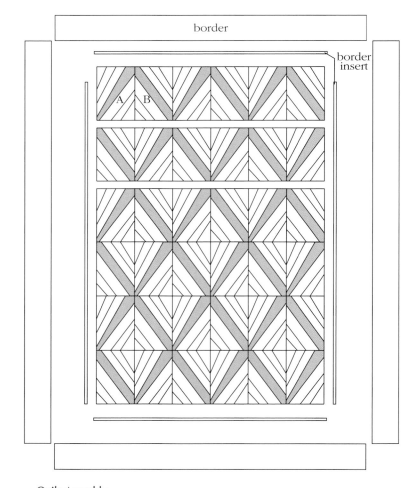

Quilt Assembly

STRING QUILTS WITH STYLE – BOBBIE AUG & SHARON NEWMAN

6 MARK QUILTING: Mark the quilting design on the quilt top (see Quilting Design below). To use the full-size quilting pattern on page 22, trace the design from the book onto tracing paper. Then, using a source of backlighting, trace the design on your fabric. Frame each floral quilting motif with quilted diamonds by quilting down the center of each string. Mark the borders in parallel diagonal lines approximately 2" apart, starting at the center of each side and working outward.

7 FINISH QUILT: Layer the quilt top, batting, and backing. Baste the layers together. After quilting by hand or machine, remove the basting and trim the batting and backing even with the quilt top. Finish the edges with 2"-wide bias binding. Add a sleeve in the back for hanging the quilt, if desired. Remember to sign and date your quilt.

Quilting Design (top left corner)

TAPESTRY
Full-Size Quilting Pattern

String Quilts with Style – Bobbie Aug & Sharon Newman

TAPESTRY
(KING SIZE)

SEWING DIRECTIONS

Follow the directions for the smaller version, on page 20, with these exceptions:

Cut additional pieces to make 96 A rectangles and 96 B rectangles. Refer to the Quilt Assembly diagram below to arrange and join the rows.

Finish with the suggested quilting. Remember to sign and date your quilt.

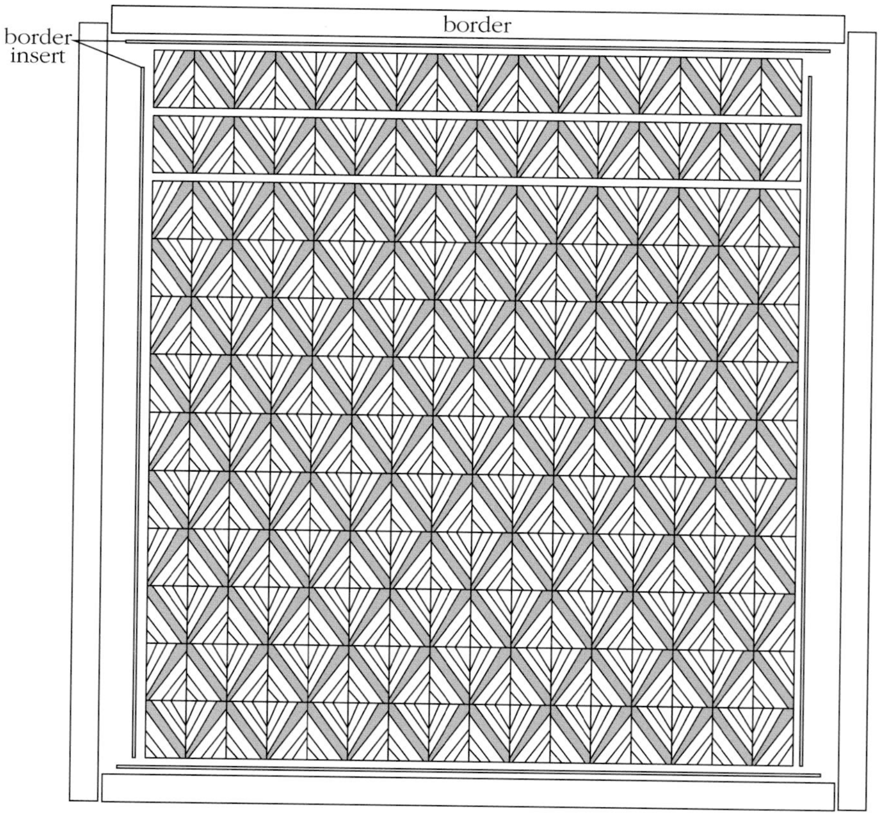

Quilt size 104" x 116"
Finished string-pieced rectangle 6" x 9"

CUTTING REQUIREMENTS

PAPER FOUNDATIONS
192 rectangles 6½" x 9½"

SCRAPS 10 yds. equivalent
Strings average 2½" wide

ACCENT FABRIC 5⅛ yds.
Center strings average 2½" wide
10 border insert strips 1½" wide, cut selvage to selvage

MITERED BORDER 3½ yds.
2 strips 4½" x 118½"
2 strips 4½" x 106½"

BINDING 1 yd.
Cut 2"-wide bias strips from 32" square

BACKING 10½ yds.
3 panels 36½" x 120"

BATTING 108" x 120"

Quilt Assembly

border

border insert

• KNOW-HOW •

String Quilts with Style – Bobbie Aug & Sharon Newman

LOOSE CHANGE

Quilt size 66½" x 82"

Finished string-pieced rectangle 3½" x 7½"

CUTTING REQUIREMENTS

PAPER FOUNDATIONS
90 rectangles 4" x 8"

SCRAPS 3½ yds. equivalent
Strings average 2" wide

SASHES, BORDERS, AND BINDING 4½ yds.
10 sashes 4" x 77½", cut parallel to selvages

2 border strips 4" x 69", cut parallel to selvages

Binding, cut 2"-wide bias strips from 27" square

BACKING 5 yds.
2 panels 36" x 86"

BATTING 70½" x 86"

LOOSE CHANGE, by Bobbie Aug; machine quilted by Janet Spencer. The bar setting gave this quilt its structure since all the fabric pieces were selected and sewn at random. This design is a variation of the classic Chinese Coins pattern. Perhaps the green sashing and border fabric calls paper money to mind.

LOOSE CHANGE

SEWING DIRECTIONS

1 **MAKE STRING-PIECED RECTANGLES:** Sew strings crosswise on the foundation rectangles. After you have filled the foundations with strings, trim them even with the edges of the paper.

2 **SEW RECTANGLES INTO STRIPS:** Sew the string-pieced rectangles together in 9 vertical strips of 10 rectangles each. Press the seam allowances downward in each row.

3 **MEASURE ROWS:** The string-pieced strips need to be within ¼" of each other in length. If the discrepancy is greater than ¼", adjust the strips by taking in or letting out the seam allowances between the rectangles. Then determine the average length of the strips.

4 **TRIM SASHING STRIPS:** The 10 sashes need to be trimmed to the average length of the string-pieced strips. Mark the half, quarter, and eighth measurements on all strips, as described for marking borders, page 85.

5 **ASSEMBLE QUILT TOP:** Starting and ending with a sash, alternate sashes and string-pieced strips (refer to the Quilt Assembly diagram). Pin and sew the strips together, matching the half, quarter, and eighth measurements. Add the border strips to the top and bottom of the quilt. Trim the border strips even with the quilt edges and remove the paper foundations.

6 **MARK QUILTING DESIGN:** It is generally easier to mark the quilt top before the quilt is layered. In this quilt, the borders and sashing strips have been quilted in a curved cable pattern. The string-pieced rows have been quilted in an angular cable design.

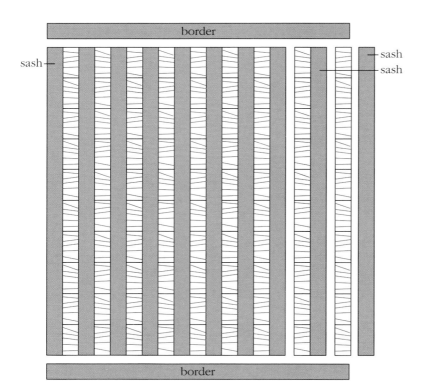

border

sash

sash

sash

border

Quilt Assembly

7 FINISH QUILT: Layer the quilt top, batting, and backing and baste the layers together. After quilting by hand or machine, remove the basting and trim the batting and backing even with the quilt top. Finish the edges with 2"-wide bias binding. Add a sleeve in the back for hanging the quilt, if desired. Remember to sign and date your quilt.

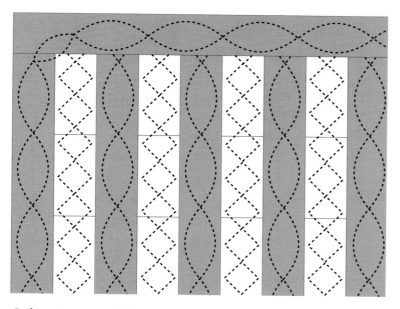

Quilting Design (top left corner)

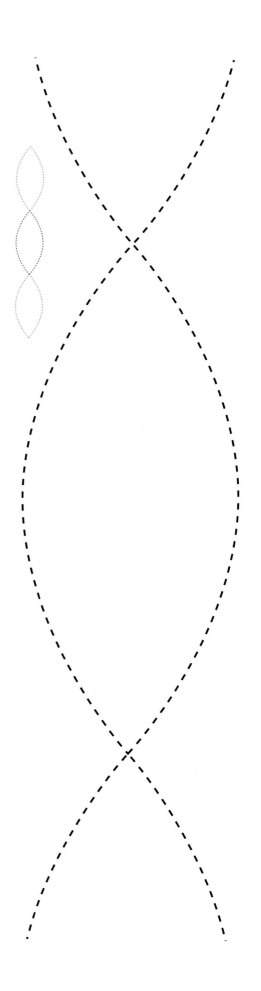

LOOSE CHANGE
Full-Size Quilting Patterns

CHURCH WINDOWS

Quilt size 67" x 99"

Finished string-pieced square 5½"

CUTTING REQUIREMENTS

PAPER FOUNDATIONS

   78 squares 6"

SCRAPS 4¾ yds. equivalent
   Strings for squares and border
      average 2½" wide

BLACK 3 yds.
   65 short sashes 1½" x 6"
   14 long sashes 1½" x 40"
   2 side sashes 1½" x 88"
   2 inner borders 1½" x 98½"
   1 inner border 1½" x 63½"
   2 outer borders 1½" x 101½"
   1 outer border 1½" x 69½"
   Binding, cut 2"-wide bias
      strips from 29" square

WIDE BORDER 2⅞ yds.
   2 strips 10" x 97½", cut par-
      allel to selvages
   1 strip 10" x 42½", cut parallel
      to selvages

BACKING 6 yds.
   2 panels 36" x 103"

BATTING 71" x 103"

CHURCH WINDOWS, by VALERIA WIMMER. Clear colors sashed with black create a stained-glass effect. Bed quilts are frequently made without top borders.

CHURCH WINDOWS

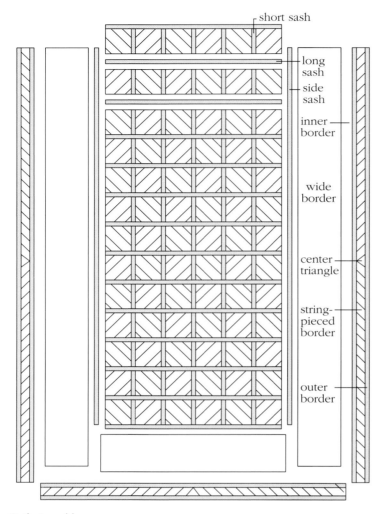

short sash

long sash

side sash

inner border

wide border

center triangle

string-pieced border

outer border

Quilt Assembly

Figure 2–2. Mark short sash seam lines on long sashes to help with matching.

SEWING DIRECTIONS

1 **MAKE STRING-PIECED SQUARES:** Sew strings diagonally on the foundations. Trim the strings even with the edges of the paper.

2 **ASSEMBLE SQUARES AND SASHING:** On a flat surface, arrange string-pieced squares in 13 rows of 6 each. Referring to the Quilt Assembly diagram and to the photograph, rotate the squares to form diamond pattern.

Place short sashes (1½" x 6") between the squares in each horizontal row. Stitch the squares and sashes together by row, pressing seam allowances toward the sashes.

Trim the long sashes (1½" x 40") equal to the average length of the sewn rows. To ensure that the squares are evenly aligned across the quilt, use a ruler to measure and mark the ¼" seam allowances at the ends of the long sashes and mark the seam lines for the vertical sashes (Figure 2–2). Matching marks, pin and sew a long sashing strip between each row and on the top and bottom of the quilt.

For the side sashes, use 5 strips 1½"-wide, cut selvage to selvage, to make 2 pieced strips 88" long. Matching half and quarter measurements, as described for marking borders, page 85, pin and sew the strips to the sides of the quilt and trim off the extra length even with the top and bottom of the quilt. Remove the paper foundations.

3 **ADD WIDE BORDER:** Matching half and quarter measurements, sew the 10" x 42½" border strip to the bottom of the quilt. Trim off extra length. In the same manner, add a long border strip to each side.

4 **ADD BORDERS:** From the black fabric, cut 13 1½"-wide strips, selvage to selvage. Sew the strips together end to end, as needed, to make the lengths listed in the Cutting Requirements for the inner and outer borders.

You will need paper foundations for the string-pieced borders. These can be made from adding-machine tape or strips of paper taped together. Make 2 foundations for the side strips, 2½" x 100½", and 1 foundation for the bottom strip, 2½" x 67½".

Fold the paper strips in half to mark the positions for the center triangles. You can place 45° diagonal lines every few inches along the foundations to help keep the strings angled as you sew (Figure 2–3).

Place a fabric for the triangle in the center of one of the border foundations and sew strings on either side of the triangle until the foundations is filled. Repeat for the other string-pieced border strips.

Referring to the Quilt Assembly diagram, sew black border strips to each side of the string-pieced strips. Remove the paper foundations from the borders. Pin and sew the combined borders to the quilt, but stop stitching ¼" form the bottom corners and backstitch. Sew the miters at the corners. At the top of the quilt, trim the border strips even with the quilt edge.

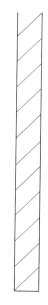

FIGURE 2–3. MARK GUIDE LINES EVERY FEW INCHES ON BORDER FOUNDATIONS.

5 MARK QUILTING DESIGN: It is generally easier to mark the quilt top before the quilt is layered. To mark the quilting design in the white border, use the full-size tulip pattern, on these pages. Trace the design onto tracing paper. Then, using a source of backlighting, trace the design on your fabric. The string-pieced squares, sashes, and borders can be quilted in the ditch.

6 FINISH QUILT: Layer the quilt top, batting, and backing, and baste the layers together. After quilting by hand or machine, remove the basting and trim the batting and backing even with the quilt top. Finish the edges with 2"-wide bias binding. Add a sleeve in the back for hanging the quilt, if desired. Remember to sign and date your quilt.

QUILTING DESIGN (bottom left corner)

CHURCH WINDOWS

Full-Size Quilting Pattern

String Quilts with Style – Bobbie Aug & Sharon Newman

CHURCH WINDOWS

Full-Size Quilting Pattern
continued

String Quilts with Style – Bobbie Aug & Sharon Newman

DOUBLE CROSS

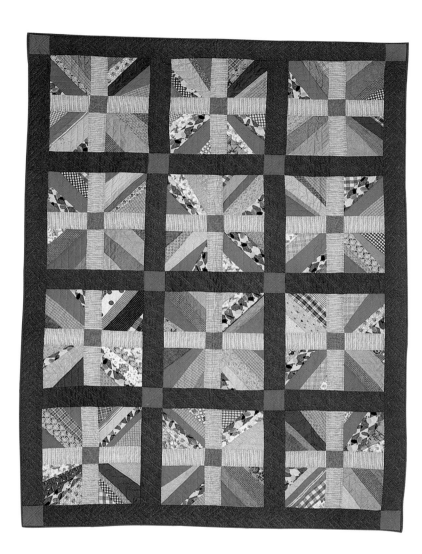

Quilt size 52½" x 69"

Finished string-pieced square 5¾"

Finished block 13½"

CUTTING REQUIREMENTS

PAPER FOUNDATIONS
48 squares 6¼"

SCRAPS 2⅜ yds. equivalent
Strings average 2¼" wide

BLUE PRINT 2 yds.
2 border strips 3½" x 65½", cut parallel to selvages
2 border strips 3½" x 49", cut parallel to selvages
17 sashes 3½" x 14"

TAN STRIPE ¾ yd.
48 sashes 2½" x 6¼"

ORANGE SOLID ¼ yd.
10 setting squares 3½"

ORANGE PRINT ¼ yd.
12 setting squares 2½"

BINDING ¾ yd.
Cut 2"-wide bias strips from 25" square

BACKING 4⅜ yds.
2 panels 29" x 73"

BATTING 56½" x 73"

DOUBLE CROSS, by TERRI ELLIS. To show that string quilting is not new, the four square units in each block in this quilt were pieced on newspaper from around 1940. The tan sashing within each block and the blue sashing that sets the blocks were chosen to enhance the original colors. This technique of double sashing is used effectively in many patterns that include small blocks.

DOUBLE CROSS

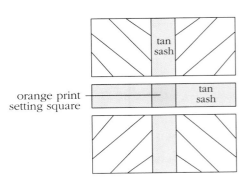

tan sash

orange print setting square

tan sash

Block Assembly

SEWING DIRECTIONS

1 MAKE STRING-PIECED SQUARES: Sew the strings on the diagonal and use an orange accent in a majority of the squares. Trim the strings even with the edges of the paper foundations.

2 SEW BLOCKS: Refer to the Block Assembly diagram and make 12 blocks, each containing 4 string-pieced squares, 4 tan stripe sashes, and 1 orange-print setting square. Be sure to check the orientation of the diagonal strings as you sew. Press seam allowances toward the sashes.

3 ASSEMBLE QUILT TOP: Arrange quilt blocks in 4 rows of 3. Sew 3½" x 14" blue sashes between the three blocks in each row (see Quilt Assembly diagram). Join 3 sashes alternately with 2 orange setting squares to make a sashing row. Make 3 rows in this manner. Sew the sashing rows in between the block rows.

4 ADD BORDERS: Mark half and quarter measurements, as described for adding borders on page 84. Before adding the long side borders, measure the quilt width and trim the top and bottom borders to this measurement. Set them aside. Stitch the long border strips to the sides of the quilt. Trim the strips even with the quilt edges. Stitch the orange setting squares to the ends of the top and bottom border strips and sew them to the quilt. Remove paper foundations.

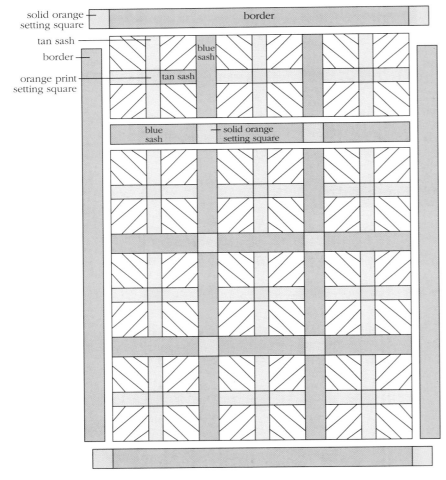

solid orange setting square

tan sash

border

orange print setting square

border

blue sash

tan sash

blue sash

solid orange setting square

Quilt Assembly

5 **MARK QUILTING DESIGN:** It is generally easier to mark the quilt top before the quilt is layered. Use a ruler to mark the various patterns shown in the Quilting Design diagram below, or quilt as desired.

6 **FINISH QUILT:** Layer the quilt top, batting, and backing. Pin or thread baste the layers together. After quilting the design, remove the basting and trim the batting and backing even with the quilt top. Bind your quilt with 2"-wide bias binding. Remember to sign and date your quilt.

Quilting Design (top left corner)

String Quilts with Style – Bobbie Aug & Sharon Newman

SQUARED STRINGS I

Quilt size 63" x 78"

Finished string-pieced square 5½"

CUTTING REQUIREMENTS

PAPER FOUNDATIONS
    50 squares 6"

SCRAPS 2¼ yds. equivalent
    Strings average 1¾" wide

BACKGROUND 3 yds.
    90 side triangles, cut from 23
        squares 9⅛"
    20 corner triangles, cut from
        10 squares 5"
    Binding, cut 2"-wide bias strips
        from 27" square

STRIPE 2½ yds.
    6 vertical sashes 4½" x 80½"

BACKING 5 yds.
    2 panels 34" x 82"

BATTING 67" x 82"

SQUARED STRINGS I, by GWEN DAVIS OBERG. While the pattern and setting of this quilt are similar to SQUARED STRINGS II (page 49), brightly colored novelty prints and a confetti-sprinkled black fabric contribute a contemporary and exciting look. An orange-peel machine-quilting design throws a definite curve into the mix.

SQUARED STRINGS I

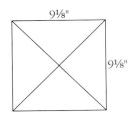

FIGURE 2–4. CUT 4 SIDE TRIANGLES FROM EACH SQUARE.

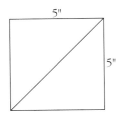

FIGURE 2–5. CUT 2 CORNER TRIANGLES FROM EACH SQUARE.

SEWING DIRECTIONS

1 **MAKE STRING-PIECED SQUARES:** Sew the strings diagonally across each paper foundation square. Trim the strings even with the edges of the paper.

2 **CUT BACKGROUND TRIANGLES:** Cut the 9⅛" squares in half diagonally twice (Figure 2–4) to make the 90 side triangles. Cut the 5" squares in half diagonally once (Figure 2–5) to make the 20 corner triangles.

3 **MAKE PIECED VERTICAL STRIPS:** Assemble the string-pieced squares and background triangles in 5 vertical strips of 10 squares each, as shown in the Quilt Assembly diagram. Sew the squares and triangles in diagonal rows, then sew the rows together to complete the strips. Please note: For ease in measuring and assembly, the triangles were cut slightly oversized. Trim each pieced strip, leaving ¼" seam allowances beyond the points all around.

4 **TRIM VERTICAL SASHES:** Measure the string-pieced strips. They should be within ¼" of each other. If they are not, you can make adjustments in the seams between the rows. Trim the sashes to match the pieced strips in length.

5 **ASSEMBLE QUILT TOP:** To keep the string-pieced squares aligned across the quilt, mark the following placement guides on the long edges of the sashes. Place the first mark 3⅞" from the top, then place marks at 7¾" intervals (see Figure 2–6). Match these marks to the square points in the string-pieced strips, then pin. (Sew with the pieced strips on top so you can see the points.) Remove paper foundations.

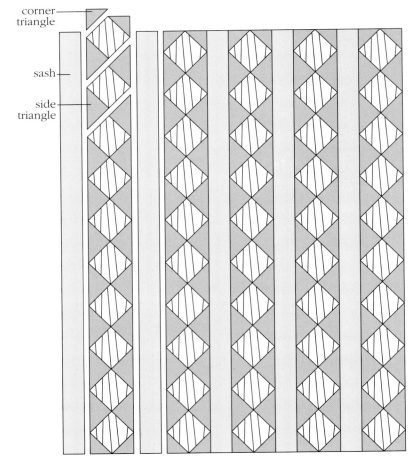

Quilt Assembly

6 **MARK QUILTING:** Mark the quilting design, if desired, before layering the quilt top, batting, and backing. To quilt as shown, trace the designs from the book onto tracing paper. Then, using a source of backlighting, trace them on your fabric (see Quilting Design).

7 **FINISH QUILT:** Layer the top, batting, and backing and baste the layers together. Stitch in the ditch around each string block and quilt along the marked lines, or as desired. Remove the basting and trim the batting and backing even with the quilt top. Finish the edges with 2"-wide bias binding. Remember to sign and date your quilt.

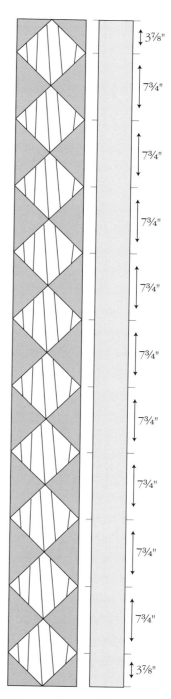

FIGURE 2–6. PLACE MATCHING MARKS ON SASHES.

QUILTING DESIGN (TOP LEFT CORNER)

SQUARED STRINGS I

place on block diagonal

FESTIVAL

Quilt size 47½" x 57½"

CUTTING REQUIREMENTS

PAPER FOUNDATIONS
    36 half-square triangles cut
        from 18 squares 8"

SCRAPS 1½ yds. equivalent
    Strings average 2¾" wide

BLACK 3⅛ yds.
    36 side triangles, cut from 9
        squares 11½"
    16 corner triangles, cut from 8
        squares 6"
    2 border strips 4" x 53"
    2 border strips 4" x 50"
    Binding, cut 2"-wide bias strips
        from 23" square

BACKING 3⅝ yds.
    2 panels 26½" x 61½"

BATTING 51½" x 61½"

FESTIVAL, by Bobbie Aug; machine quilted by Janet Spencer. Sharp zigzags of a classic Streak o' Lightning pattern always seem more complex than they really are, and the string-pieced triangles add to the amazing effects. Rich, bright colors set against a black background make this quilt visually exciting.

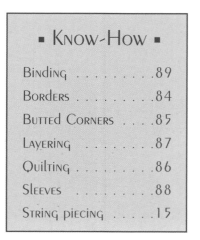

FESTIVAL

SEWING DIRECTIONS

1 MAKE STRING-PIECED TRIANGLES: Sew the strings more or less perpendicular to the base of the triangle. Trim the strings even with the edges of the paper foundations.

2 CUT BACKGROUND TRIANGLES: Cut the 11½" squares in half diagonally twice (Figure 2–7) to make the 36 side triangles. Cut the 6" squares in half diagonally once (Figure 2–8) to make the 16 corner triangles.

3 ASSEMBLE QUILT TOP: Sew the string-pieced and side triangles in vertical strips as shown in the Quilt Assembly diagram. Add the corner triangles to square off each strip. Please note: For ease in measuring and assembly, the side and corner triangles were cut slightly oversized. Trim each pieced strip, leaving ¼" seam allowances beyond the points all around. Sew the strips together.

4 ADD BORDERS: Matching half and quarter measurements (see Adding Borders, page 84), sew the long border strips to the sides and trim any extra length even with the quilt edges. In the same manner, add borders to the top and bottom. Remove paper foundations.

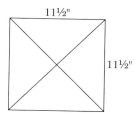

FIGURE 2–7. CUT 4 SIDE TRIANGLES FROM EACH SQUARE.

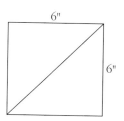

FIGURE 2–8. CUT 2 CORNER TRIANGLES FROM EACH SQUARE.

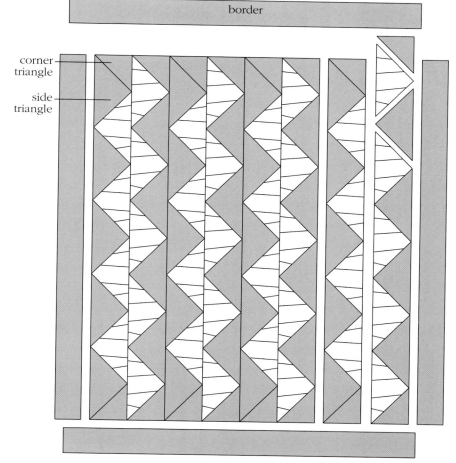

Quilt Assembly

FESTIVAL

5 **MARK QUILTING:** It is generally easier to mark the quilt top before the quilt is layered. As shown, the quilting pattern echoes the zigzag lines of the patchwork. Mark the strips and extend the parallel lines into the border. Refer to the Quilting Design diagram.

6 **FINISH QUILT:** Layer the quilt top, batting, and backing. Baste the layers together. After quilting the design, remove the basting and trim the batting and backing even with the quilt top. Bind the quilt with 2"-wide bias binding. Remember to sign and date your quilt.

QUILTING DESIGN (TOP LEFT CORNER)

FESTIVAL
(DOUBLE / QUEEN SIZE)

SEWING DIRECTIONS

Follow the directions for the smaller quilt, on page 45, but arrange setting and string-pieced triangles as shown in the double/queen Quilt Assembly diagram below.

Finish quilt with the suggested quilting. Remember to sign and date your quilt.

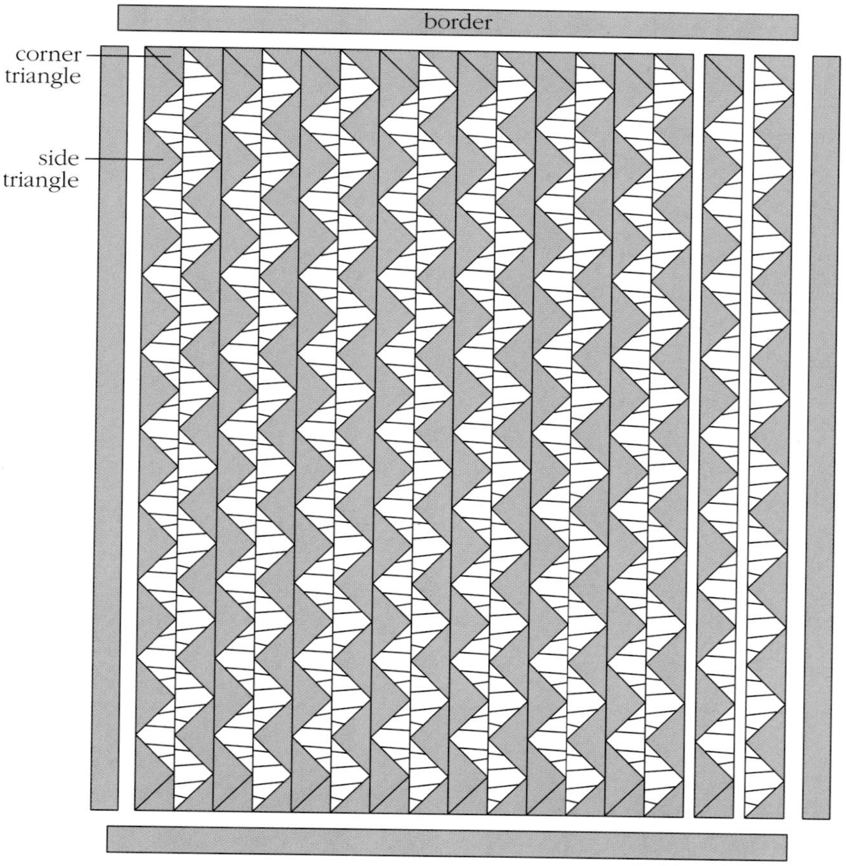

Quilt size 89" x 109"

CUTTING REQUIREMENTS

PAPER FOUNDATIONS

152 half-square triangles cut from 76 squares 8"

SCRAPS 6⅛ yds. equivalent

Strings average 2¾" wide

BLACK 8⅛ yds.

152 side triangles cut from 38 squares 11½"

32 corner triangles cut from 16 squares 6"

2 border strips 4½" x 103½"

2 border strips 4½" x 91½"

Binding, cut 2"-wide bias strips from 31" square

BACKING 10 yds.

3 panels 31½" x 113"

BATTING 93" x 113"

Quilt Assembly for double / queen

String Quilts with Style – Bobbie Aug & Sharon Newman

SQUARED STRINGS II

Quilt size 24" x 25"

Finished string-pieced square 3½"

CUTTING REQUIREMENTS

PAPER FOUNDATIONS
   15 squares 4"

SCRAPS ½ yd. equivalent
   Strings average 1½" wide

BACKGROUND ⅜ yd.
   24 side triangles, cut from 6
      squares 6¼"
   12 corner triangles, cut from 6
      squares 3½"

PLAID 1 yd.
   4 vertical sashes 2¾" x 27½"
   Binding, cut 2"-wide bias strips
      from 17" square

BACKING ⅞ yd.
   1 panel 28" x 29"

BATTING 28" x 29"

SQUARED STRINGS II, by GWEN DAVIS OBERG. The country folk-art look of this small quilt is the result of combining beige, red, and green plaids. Because the strings are skewed, the plaids also seem skewed. Combined with the on-point setting, this fresh and lively quilt is full of visual movement. The hand quilting adds plenty of charm.

SQUARED STRINGS II

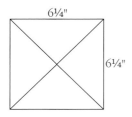

FIGURE 2–9. CUT 4 SIDE TRIANGLES FROM EACH SQUARE.

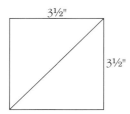

FIGURE 2–10. CUT 2 CORNER TRIANGLES FROM EACH SQUARE.

SEWING DIRECTIONS

1 MAKE STRING-PIECED SQUARES: Sew the strings diagonally across each paper foundation square. Trim the strings even with the edges of the paper.

2 CUT BACKGROUND TRIANGLES: Cut the 6½" squares diagonally twice (Figure 2–9) to make the 24 side triangles. Cut the 3½" squares in half diagonally (Figure 2–10) to make the 12 corner triangles.

3 MAKE PIECED VERTICAL STRIPS: Assemble the string-pieced squares and background triangles in 3 vertical strips of 5 squares each, as shown in the Quilt Assembly diagram. Sew the squares and triangles in diagonal rows, then sew the rows together to complete the strips. Please note: For ease in measuring and assembly, the triangles were cut slightly oversized. Trim each pieced strip, leaving ¼" seam allowances beyond the points all around.

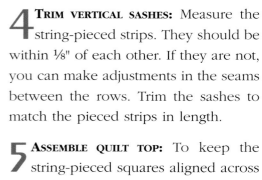

4 TRIM VERTICAL SASHES: Measure the string-pieced strips. They should be within ⅛" of each other. If they are not, you can make adjustments in the seams between the rows. Trim the sashes to match the pieced strips in length.

5 ASSEMBLE QUILT TOP: To keep the string-pieced squares aligned across the quilt, mark the following placement guides on the long edges of the sashes. Place the first mark 2½" from the top, then place four marks at 5" intervals (see Figure 2–11). Match these marks to the square points in the string-pieced strips, then pin. (Sew with the pieced strips on top so you can see the points.) Remove paper foundations.

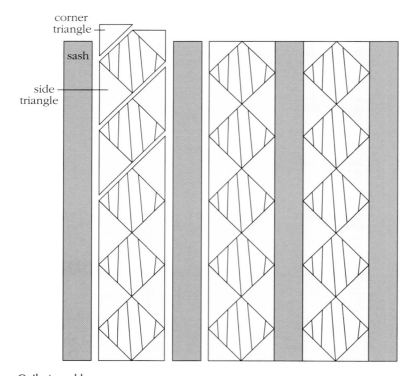

Quilt Assembly

6 **MARK QUILTING:** Mark the quilting design, if desired, before layering the quilt top, batting, and backing. A simple square within a square pattern was quilted across the sashing strips between the string-pieced squares.

7 **FINISH QUILT:** Layer the top, batting, and backing, and baste the layers together. Stitch in the ditch around each string block and quilt along the marked lines, or as desired. Remove the basting and trim the batting and backing even with the quilt top. Finish the edges with 2"-wide bias binding. Remember to sign and date your quilt.

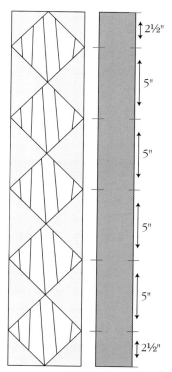

FIGURE 2–11. PLACE MATCHING MARKS ON SASHES.

Quilting Design (top left corner)

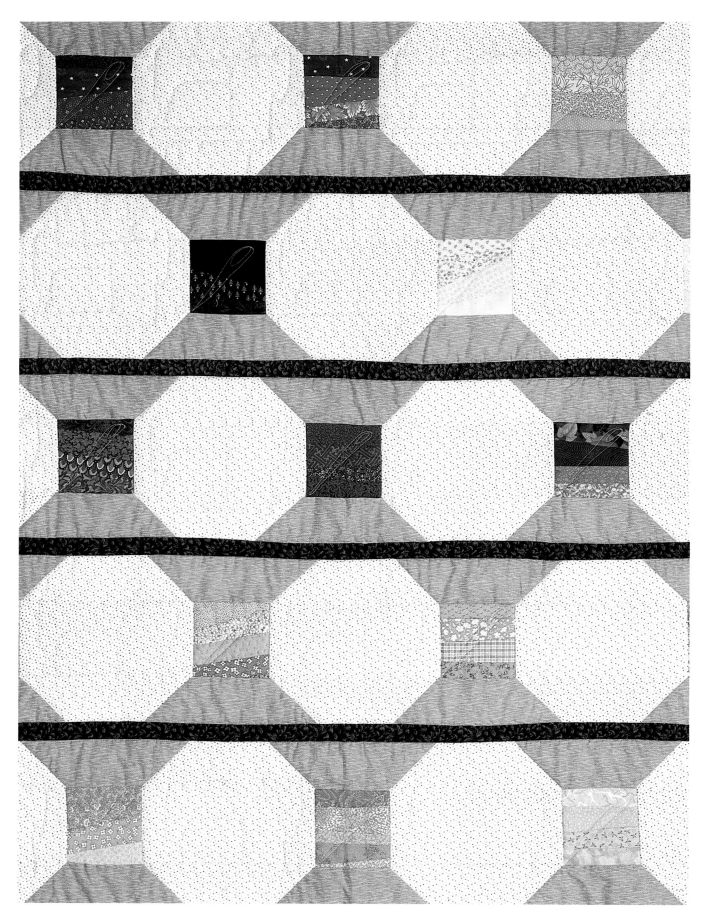

String Quilts with Style – Bobbie Aug & Sharon Newman

SPOOLS

Quilt size 82" x 107"

Finished string-pieced square 4"

CUTTING REQUIREMENTS

PAPER FOUNDATIONS

    55 squares 4½" x 4½"

SCRAPS 1⅝ yds. equivalent

    Strings average 1½" wide

WHITE 4¼ yds.

    90 pattern A cut from 3" strips

    20 triangles (B), cut 10 3⅜"
        squares once diagonally

    10 small rectangles (C) 3" x
        4½"

    55 large rectangles (D) 4½" x 9½"

    10 E cut from 3" strips

    10 Er cut from 3" strips

LIGHT BROWN 2⅛ yds.

    110 spool caps (A) cut from 3"
        strips

DARK BROWN 3¼ yds.

    9 sashing strips 1½" x 76½"

    2 border strips 4½" x 101½",
        cut parallel to selvages

    2 border strips 4½" x 84½", cut
        parallel to selvages

    Cut (19) 2"-wide bias binding
        from remaining fabric.

BACKING 6½ yds.

    2 panels 43½" x 111"

SPOOLS, by SHARON NEWMAN; MACHINE QUILTED by Allison BAYER.
Shaded strings create the threads on these spools, stacked neatly by color. A quilted image of a sewing needle can be found in the threads of each spool, and a quilted sewing machine image fills the background areas between the spools.

■ KNOW-HOW ■

SPOOLS

SEWING DIRECTIONS

1 **MAKE STRING-PIECED SQUARES:** Sew strings of the same color family on each paper foundation square. Trim the strings even with the edges of the paper.

2 **MAKE TEMPLATES:** Trace pattern pieces A, and E & Er on template plastic and cut out on the solid line. Use templates to mark the A, E, and Er patches on your fabrics. Cut out all pieces listed under Cutting Requirements, as needed.

3 **PIECE SPOOL ROWS:** Following the Quilt Assembly diagram, make 5 each of spool rows 1 and 2.

4 **ASSEMBLE QUILT TOP:** Arrange rows of spools following the Quilt Assembly diagram. Place sashing between rows of spools and stitch all the rows together. Trim the sashing ends even with the edges of the quilt.

5 **ADD BORDERS:** Matching half and quarter measurements (see borders, page 84), sew borders to the sides and trim any extra length even with the quilt edges. In the same manner, add borders to the top and bottom. Remove paper foundations.

6 **MARK QUILTING:** Mark the quilting design, if desired, before layering the quilt top, batting, and backing. To quilt as shown, transfer the pattern for the sewing machine to the background octagons. Transfer the needle design, on a slight diagonal, over the "thread" area on each string-pieced patch.

Quilt Assembly

7 **FINISH QUILT:** Layer the quilt top, batting, and backing, and baste the layers together. Quilt marked areas. Quilt in the ditch to outline each spool shape. This quilt features a continuous-line pattern of vines and leaves in the borders. It was machine sewn freehand with a darning foot. Practice this technique on a scrap sandwich of fabric and batting before sewing it on your quilt. Bind the quilt with 2"-wide bias binding. Remember to sign and date your quilt.

SEW STRINGS OF THE SAME COLOR FAMILY IN EACH SQUARE.

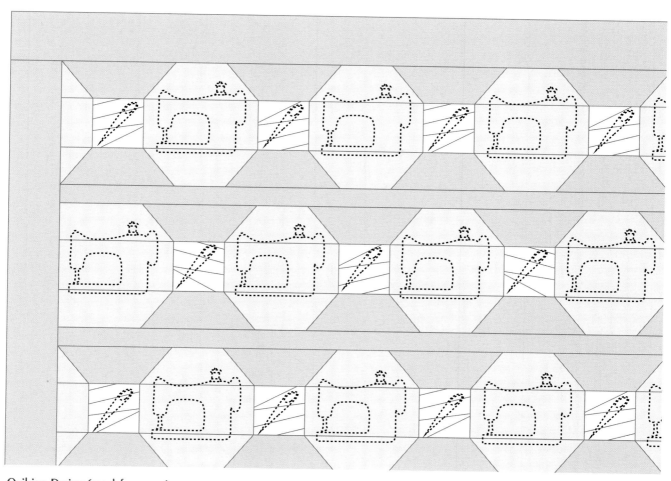

Quilting Design (top left corner)

SPOOLS

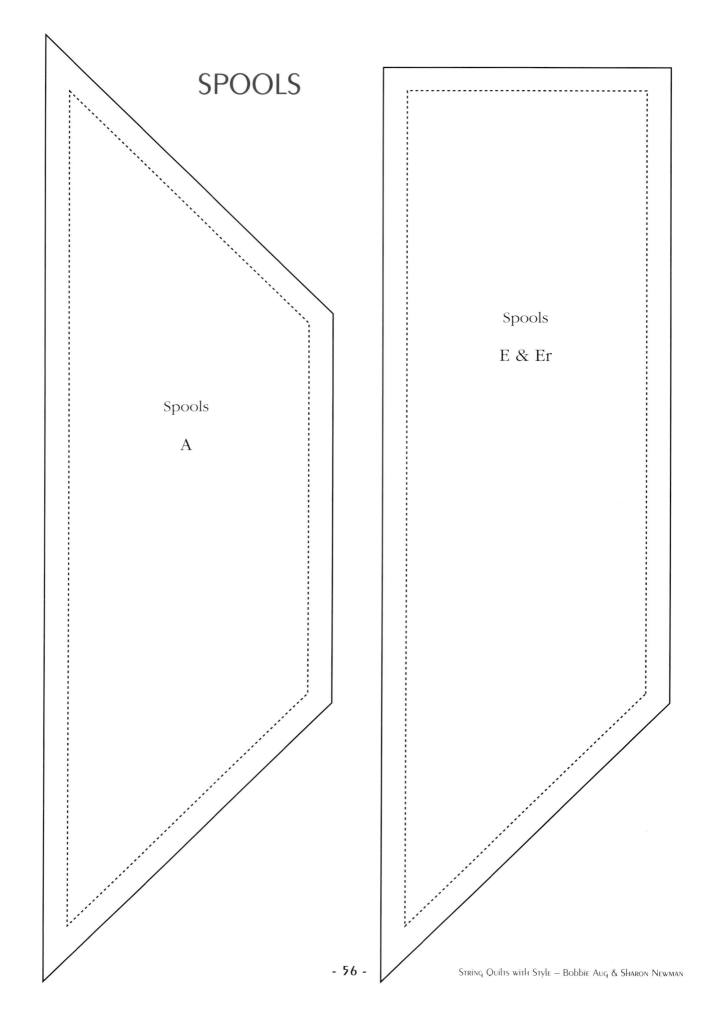

Spools

A

Spools

E & Er

STRING QUILTS WITH STYLE — BOBBIE AUG & SHARON NEWMAN

SPOOLS

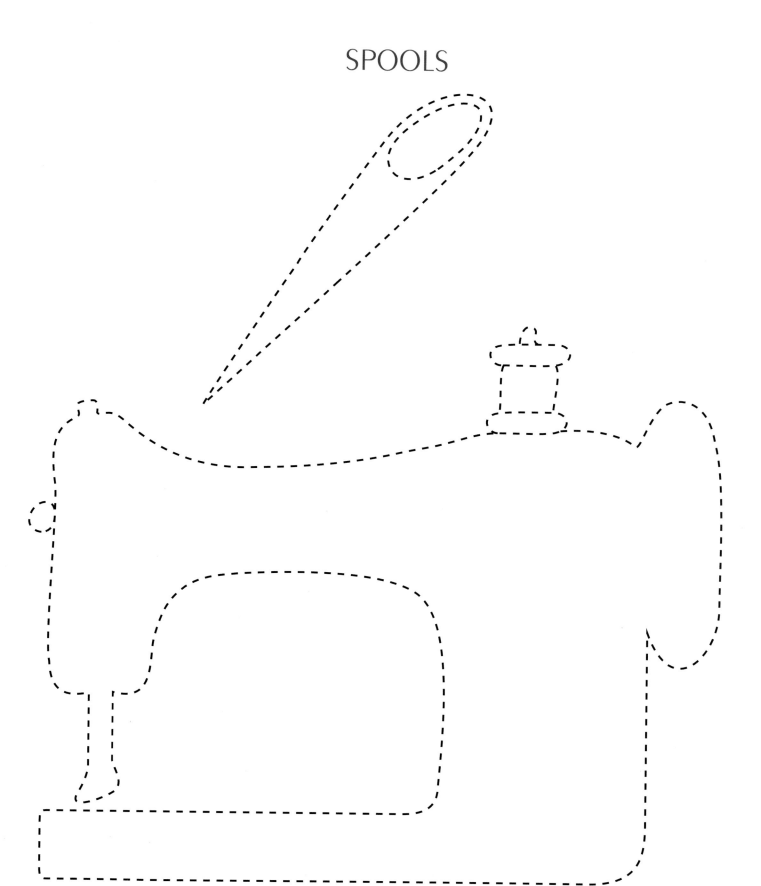

Full-Size Quilting Patterns

STRING QUILTS WITH STYLE – BOBBIE AUG & SHARON NEWMAN

CHAPELHOUSE LANES

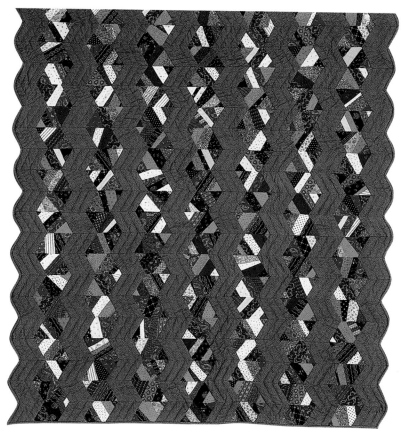

Quilt size 46" x 53"
Finished diamond 3" each side

CUTTING REQUIREMENTS

PAPER FOUNDATIONS
140 diamonds, pattern A

SCRAPS 2½ yds. equivalent
Strings average 1½" wide

BACKGROUND 1¾ yds.
160 diamonds, pattern A
(optional) end triangles, 20 B
and 20 Br (see larger quilt,
page 62)

BINDING ⅞ yd.
Binding, cut 2"-wide bias strips
from 23" square

BACKING 3⅜ yds.
2 panels 25½" x 57"

BATTING 50" x 57"

CHAPELHOUSE LANES, by SHARON NEWMAN; Hand quilted by PREEMILA JESSON. Like the FESTIVAL quilt, page 43, this quilt features strong zigzags. This time, however, the pattern is based on a traditional diamond shape. String-pieced and plain diamonds are combined in horizontal rows but produce a vertical design.

CHAPELHOUSE LANES

SEWING DIRECTIONS

1 MAKE STRING-PIECED DIAMONDS: Sew strings crosswise on the paper foundations and trim them even with the edges of the paper.

2 ASSEMBLE DIAMONDS INTO ROWS: Alternating setting diamonds with string-pieced diamonds, as shown for Row 1 in Figure 2–12, stitch 15 diamonds together. Make 10 rows like this. Sew another row the same length but with the diamonds tilted in the opposite direction, Figure 2–13. Make 10 of these rows. (Add 20 B and 20 Br triangles to the ends of the rows, if you like; see double-bed size, page 62.)

3 ASSEMBLE QUILT TOP: Arrange the rows on a flat surface, as shown in the Quilt Assembly diagram. Check to see that the diamonds are oriented correctly to produce the design. This is the time to fix any rows that are facing the wrong way. Stitch the rows together in pairs, taking care to match the seams to create the zigzag pattern. Stitch the pairs of rows together to complete the quilt top. Remove the paper foundations.

4 MARK QUILTING DESIGN: It is generally easier to mark the quilt top before the quilt is layered. In Chapelhouse Lanes, the setting diamonds have been quilted in two parallel lines, echoing the zigzag pattern. A single vertical line of quilting runs along the center of each string-pieced diamond. These zigzag quilting lines run counter to those in the setting diamonds (see Quilting Design).

5 FINISH QUILT: Layer the quilt top, batting, and backing, and baste the layers together. After quilting the design, remove the basting and trim the batting and backing even with the quilt top. Finish the edges with bias binding. Remember to sign and date your quilt.

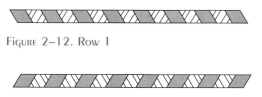

FIGURE 2–12. Row 1

FIGURE 2–13. Row 2

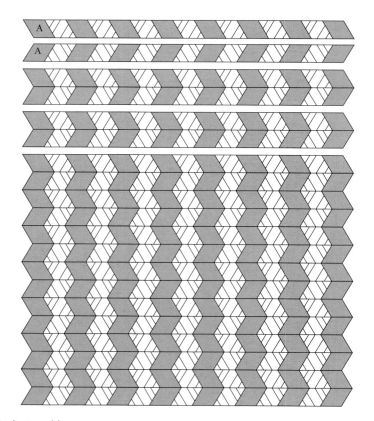

QUILT ASSEMBLY

CHAPELHOUSE LANES

Quilting Design (top left corner)

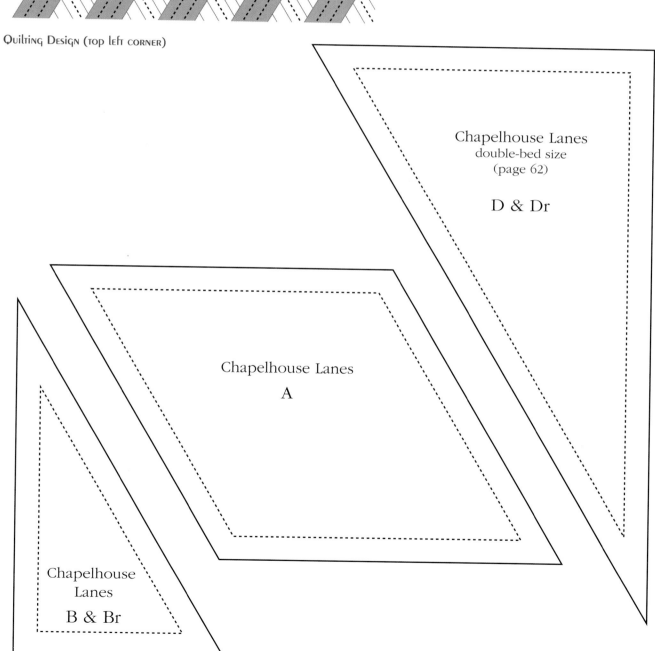

Chapelhouse Lanes
double-bed size
(page 62)

D & Dr

Chapelhouse Lanes

A

Chapelhouse
Lanes

B & Br

CHAPELHOUSE LANES
(DOUBLE-BED SIZE)

Quilt size 78" x 100"

Finished diamond 5¾" each side

CUTTING REQUIREMENTS

PAPER FOUNDATIONS

140 diamonds, pattern C

SCRAPS 5½ yds. equivalent

Strings average 2½" wide

BACKGROUND 3¾ yds.

120 diamonds, pattern C

20 triangles, pattern D

20 triangles, pattern Dr

BINDING 1 yd.

Binding, cut 2"-wide bias strips from 29" square

BACKING 7¼ yds.

3 panels 35" x 82"

BATTING 82" x 104"

SEWING DIRECTIONS

Follow the directions for the smaller version, with these exceptions: Use template C for all string-pieced and setting diamonds and put 13 diamonds in each row. Use wider strings, in scale with the larger paper foundations. Use the D & Dr triangles to square off the ends of the rows of diamonds. Refer to the Quilt Assembly diagram below to arrange and join the rows. Remember to sign and date your quilt.

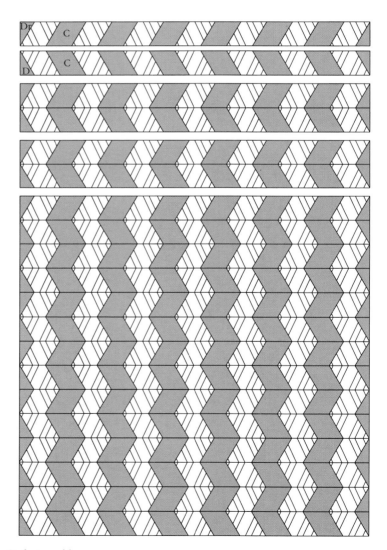

Quilt Assembly

CHAPELHOUSE LANES
(DOUBLE-BED SIZE)

The D & Dr patch is on page 61.

Chapelhouse Lanes
double-bed size

C

Quilting Design (top left corner)

String Quilts with Style – Bobbie Aug & Sharon Newman

DOS STARS

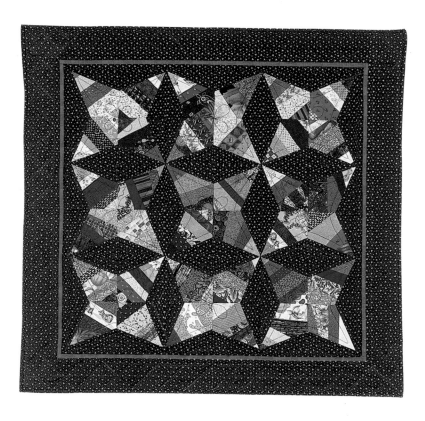

Quilt size 33½" square
Finished block 8½"

CUTTING REQUIREMENTS

PAPER FOUNDATIONS
   36 kites, pattern A

SCRAPS 1 yd. equivalent
   Strings average 2" wide

ACCENT FABRIC ¼ yd.
   4 border insert strips 1½" wide
      cut selvage to selvage

BACKGROUND 1⅝ yds.
   36 B and 36 Br triangles, cut
      from rectangles 2⅜" x 5⅞"
   2 inner borders 1½" x 30"
   2 inner borders 1½" x 28"
   2 outer borders 3½" x 36"
   2 outer borders 3½" x 30"
   Binding, cut 2"-wide bias strips
      from 19" square

BACKING 1⅛ yds.
   1 panel 37½" square

BATTING 37½" square

DOS STARS, by JALINDA MARLAR; MACHINE QUILTED by JANET SPENCER. The dark background, set against the vibrant colors of the string-pieced stars, creates a secondary star design. The inside border helps to contain the lively stars while adding excitement to the quilt.

DOS STARS

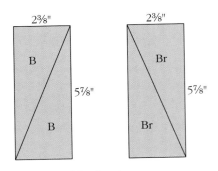

FIGURE 2–14. CUT 18 OF EACH.

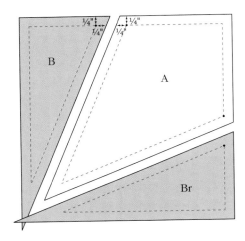

FIGURE 2–15. MARK PATCHES AS SHOWN TO HELP IN MATCHING.

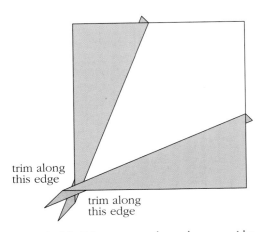

FIGURE 2–16. TRIM SQUARES ONLY ON THESE TWO SIDES.

SEWING DIRECTIONS

1 **MAKE STRING-PIECED KITES:** Sew the strings across the kite shapes. Trim the strings even with the edges of the paper.

2 **SEW STAR BLOCKS:** For the B patches, cut 18 of the rectangles in half along one diagonal and the other 18 rectangles on the other diagonal (Figure 2–14). To help with matching, on all A and B patches, mark the seam intersections as shown in Figure 2–15. Note: for ease of measuring and cutting, the B patches are slightly oversize. They will be trimmed after they are sewn.

Sew a B and a Br to each string-pieced kite to make a square unit. On the edges of the units adjacent to the kite points, trim the squares to 4¾" (Figure 2–16). Be careful to keep the kite units true as you trim. Sew 4 kite units together to make a star block (Figure 2–17). Make 9 star blocks.

3 **ASSEMBLE QUILT TOP:** Sew blocks in rows of 3 each, pressing the seam allowances in one direction for rows 1 and 3 and in the opposite direction for row 2. Pin the rows together, matching the seams, and stitch, easing any slight fullness. Press the seam allowances between rows all in one direction.

4 **ADD INNER BORDERS:** Matching half and quarter measurements, as described for Adding Borders on page 84, pin and sew a 1½" x 28" border strip to each side of the quilt. Trim the extra length even with the quilt edges. In a like manner, sew the 1½" x 30" border strips to the top and bottom. Remove paper foundations.

5 **ADD BORDER INSERT:** Measure the length and width of the quilt through the center to determine the exact lengths needed for the border inserts. Sew the 4 border insert strips together to make the lengths needed. Baste the insert strips to the quilt.

6 **ATTACH OUTER BORDERS:** Matching half and quarter measurements, sew a 3½" x 30" border strip to each side of the quilt. Trim off extra length. Then sew the 3½" x 36" border strips to the top and bottom and trim.

DOS STARS

7 **MARK QUILTING:** It is generally easier to mark the quilt top before the quilt is layered. Refer to the Quilting Design diagram, on the next page, which shows one-quarter of the quilt. The string-pieced stars are outline quilted and have a four-petal flower in the center. The borders feature a diamond cable design.

8 **FINISH QUILT:** Layer the quilt top, batting, and backing, and baste the layers together. After quilting the design, remove the basting and trim the batting and backing even with the quilt top. Finish the edges with 2"-wide bias binding. Remember to sign and date your quilt.

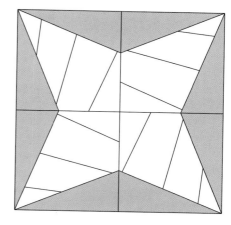

FIGURE 2–17. SEW 4 UNITS TO MAKE STAR block.

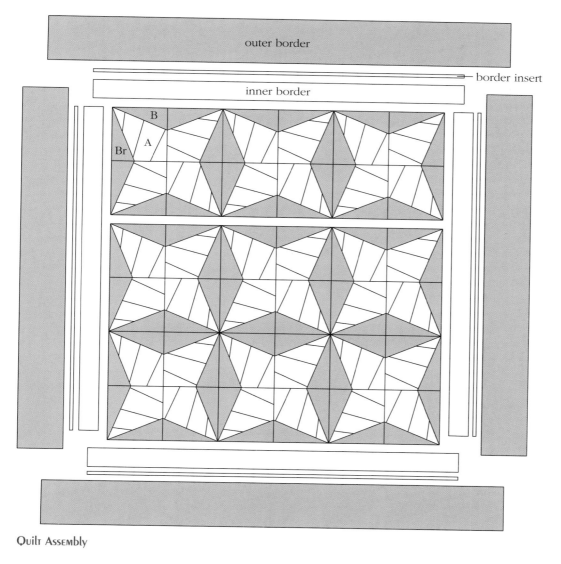

Quilt Assembly

DOS STARS

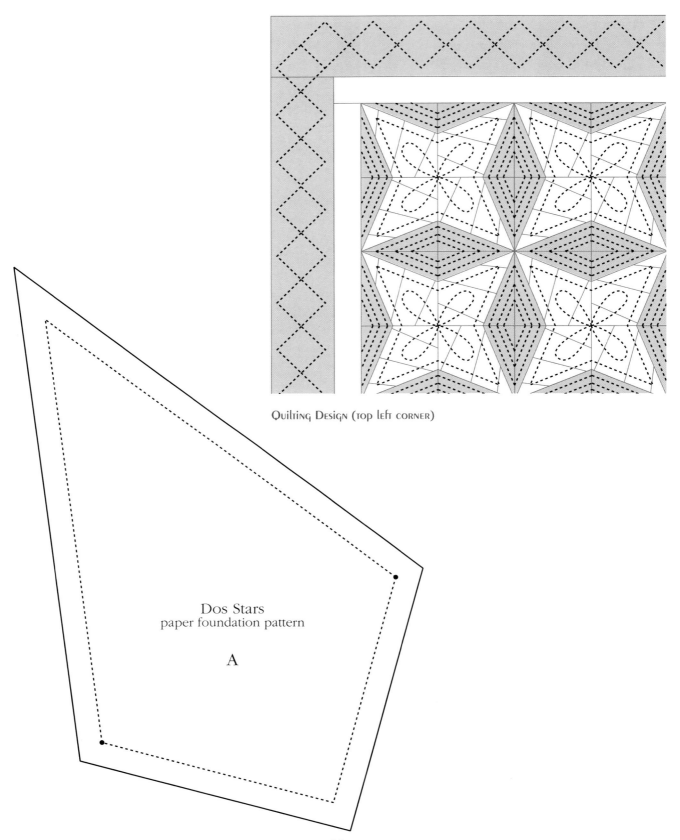

Quilting Design (top left corner)

Dos Stars
paper foundation pattern

A

DOS STARS

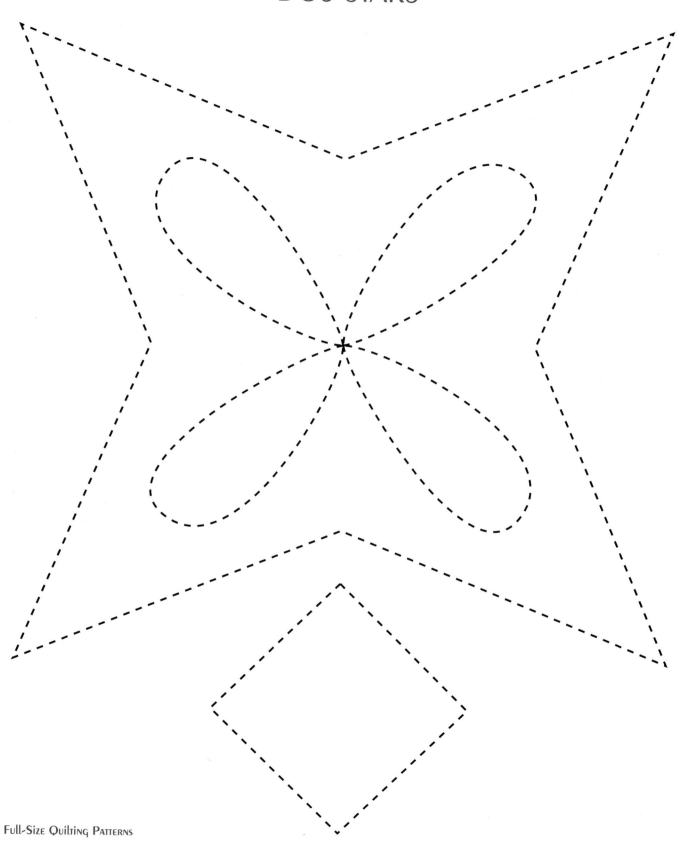

Full-Size Quilting Patterns

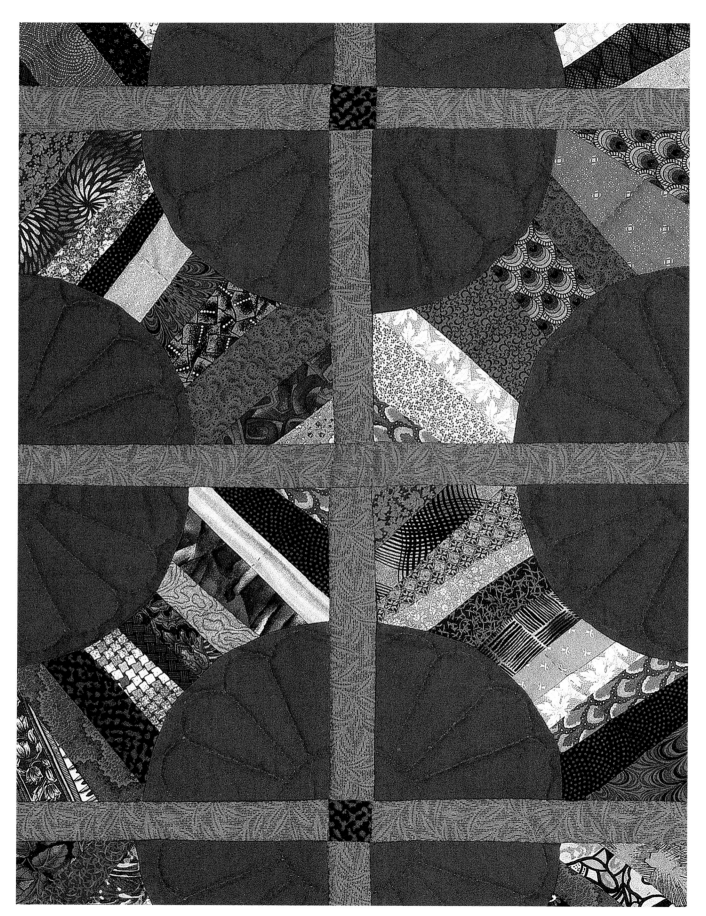

String Quilts with Style – Bobbie Aug & Sharon Newman

PURPLE PASSION

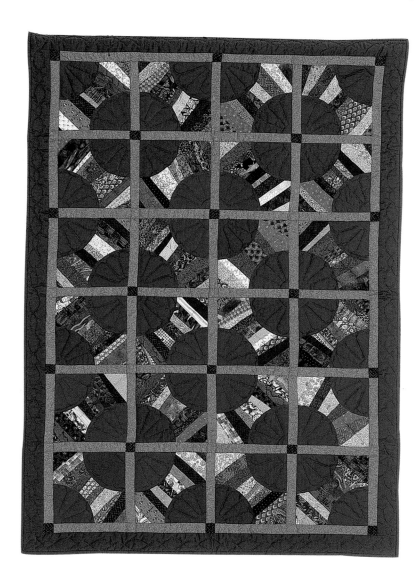

Quilt size 37" x 53"

Finished block 7"

CUTTING REQUIREMENTS

PAPER FOUNDATIONS
  24 pattern A

SCRAPS 1¼ yds.
  Strings average 1¾" wide

PURPLE 2 yds.
  2 borders 2½" x 51½"
  2 borders 2½" x 39½"
  48 pattern B
  Binding, cut 2"-wide bias strips
    from 22" square

TEAL ⅝ yd.
  17 sashes 1½" x 15½"
  24 sashes 1½" x 7½"

SETTING POSTS ⅛ yd.
  18 squares 1½"

BACKING 1¾ yds.
  1 panel 41" x 57"

BATTING 41" x 57"

PURPLE PASSION, by SHARON NEWMAN; hand quilted by SANDRA BENNETT. A curvy design with a string-pieced center is a version of the Robbing Peter to Pay Paul pattern, which can be arranged in several settings. Here, the blocks are grouped to form circles, seemingly overlaid by the lattice sashing. Decorative fan quilting emphasizes, unifies, and enhances the background pieces.

PURPLE PASSION

SEWING DIRECTIONS

1 **MAKE STRING-PIECED SHAPES:** Sew strings across shapes. Trim the strings even with the edges of the paper. To help with matching, mark the seam intersections (dots) on patterns A & B, pages 74 and 75. To produce smooth curved edges, you will need to remove the paper foundations before sewing the A and B pieces together.

2 **SEW BLOCKS:** Stitch the background B pieces to the string-pieced shapes as follows: Fold an A and a B piece in half to find the centers of the curves. Finger-crease folds to mark them. With right sides together, pin the A and B patches together, matching centers and one end (seam intersection) of the curve. Ease the fullness around that half of the curve and pin as needed.

Begin stitching at the edge. Sew to the center pin and stop. Match the other side of the curve; ease and pin as needed. Continue sewing to the end of the seam. Press the seam allowances toward the background, clipping as necessary. Make 24 blocks.

3 **SEW BLOCK ROWS:** Arrange the blocks in rows, rotating them to form the circular pattern (see Quilt Assembly diagram). Sew 3 short (1½" x 7½") sashing strips between the 4 blocks in each row. Press seam allowances toward the blocks.

4 **MAKE SASH ROWS:** There are two different sash rows. Row 1 contains 2 long sashes and 1 setting square (see Quilt Assembly diagram). Make 4.

Quilt Assembly

PURPLE PASSION

For Row 2, sew 2 short sashes, 2 setting squares, and 1 long sash as shown. Make 3.

5 ASSEMBLE QUILT TOP: Referring to the Quilt Assembly diagram, arrange block rows and sashing rows as shown. Sew the rows together.

6 SEW SIDE SASHES: Make side sashes from 3 long sashes and 4 setting squares as shown. Join these units to the sides of the quilt top. Press seam allowances toward the pieced blocks.

7 ADD BORDERS: Matching half and quarter measurements, as described for Adding Borders on page 84, stitch the long border strips to the sides of the quilt. Trim the strips even with the quilt edges. Repeat for the top and bottom borders.

8 MARK QUILTING DESIGN: Mark the quilting design, if desired. To quilt as shown, transfer the fan motif, on page 75, to each background patch.

9 FINISH QUILT: Layer the quilt top, batting, and backing. Pin or thread baste the layers together. Quilt the fan design as marked, then quilt a single straight line along the center of each string-pieced shape, from point to point. Quilt sashing strips and sashing squares in the ditch. Bind the quilt with 2"-wide bias binding. Remember to sign and date your quilt.

QUILTING DESIGN (TOP LEFT CORNER)

PURPLE PASSION

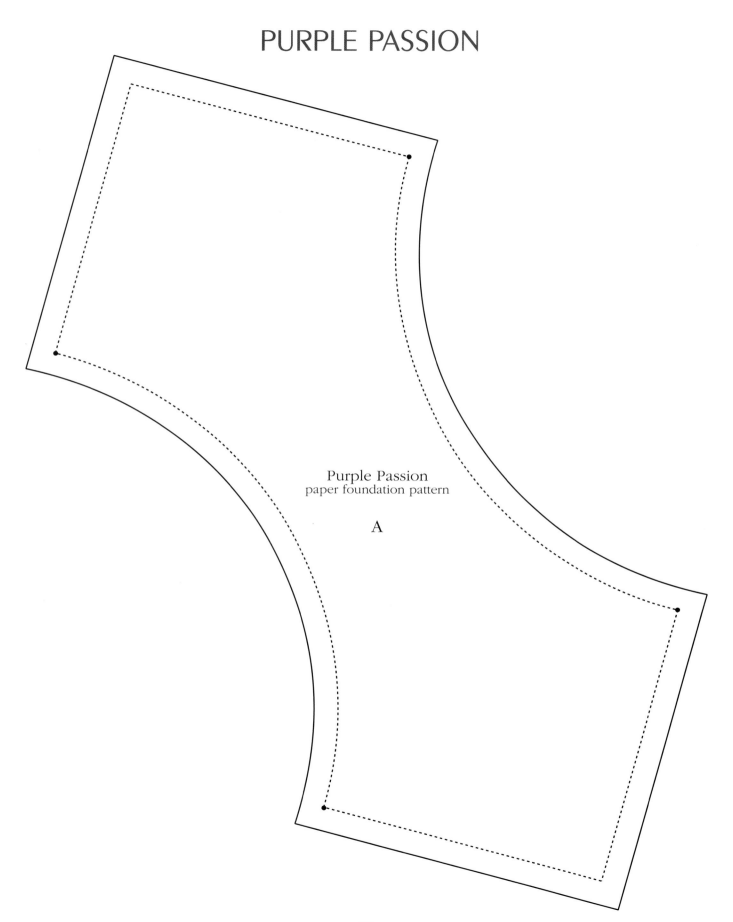

Purple Passion
paper foundation pattern

A

PURPLE PASSION

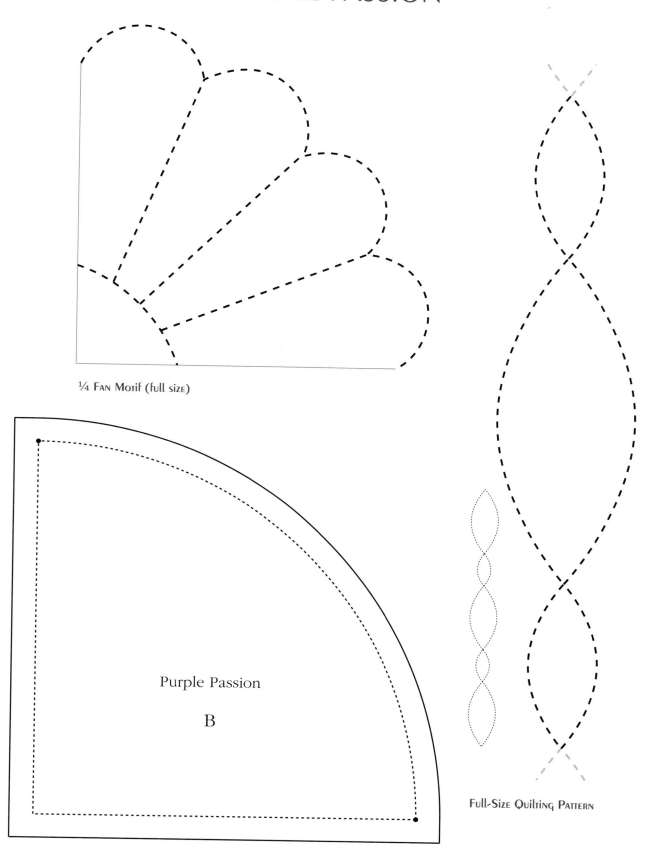

¼ Fan Motif (full size)

Purple Passion

B

Full-Size Quilting Pattern

PURPLE PASSION
(QUEEN SIZE)

Quilt Size 89" x 105"

Finished block 7"

CUTTING REQUIREMENTS

PAPER FOUNDATIONS

120 pattern A

SCRAPS 6¼ yds.

Strings average 1¾" wide

PURPLE 6 yds.

2 borders 4½" x 99½"

2 borders 4½" x 91½"

240 pattern B

Binding, cut 2"-wide
    bias strips from 31"
    square

TEAL 2¼ yds.

71 sashes 1½" x 15½"

120 sashes 1½" x 7½"

SETTING SQUARES ¼ yd.

72 squares 1½"

BACKING 9⅝ yds.

3 panels 31½" x 109"

BATTING 93" x 109"

SEWING DIRECTIONS

Follow the directions for the smaller quilt, but arrange the blocks 10 across and 12 down. Refer to the Quilt Assembly diagram for constructing sashes. Remember to sign and date your quilt.

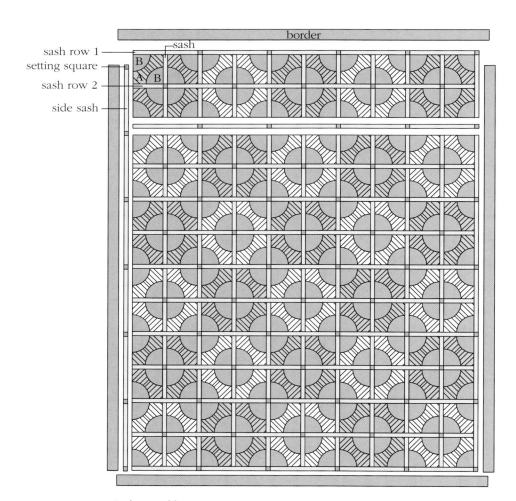

Quilt Assembly

LONE STAR

Quilt size 50" square
Finished diamond 6½" each side

CUTTING REQUIREMENTS
PAPER FOUNDATIONS
32 diamonds

SCRAPS 2 yds. equivalent
Strings average 2" wide

BACKGROUND 1¾ yds.
4 corner squares 16"
4 side triangles cut from 1
square 24"

BINDING ¾ yds.
Cut 2"-wide bias strips from
23" square

BACKING 3⅛ yds.
2 panels 27½" x 54"

BATTING 54" square

LONE STAR, by Kay Gilbert. The use of solid-colored strings within the diamonds creates quiet spaces for some charming little quilting motifs, scattered inside the star. A neutral gingham background sets off the many string fabrics and provides a good backdrop for the traditional shell quilting. All the quilting is by hand.

LONE STAR

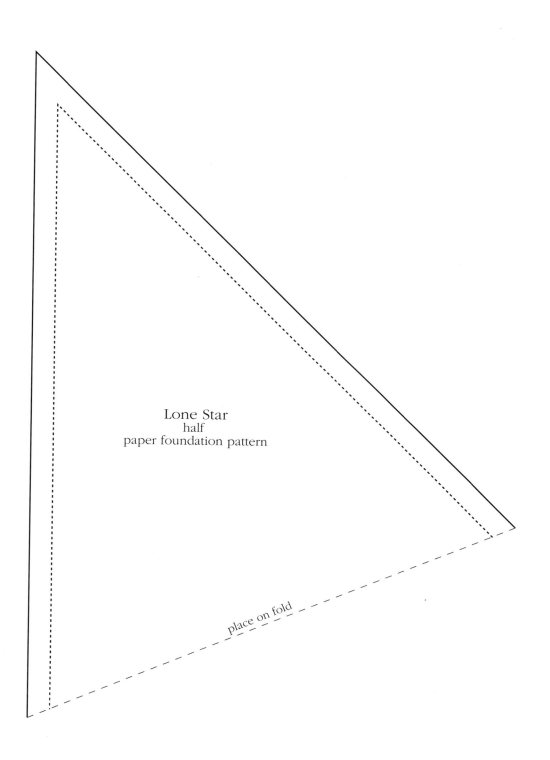

Lone Star
half
paper foundation pattern

place on fold

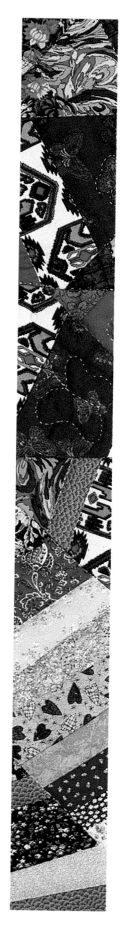

LONE STAR

FIGURE 2–18. Two-diamond unit.

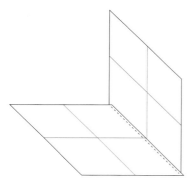

FIGURE 2–19. Large diamond.

FIGURE 2–20. Quarter star.

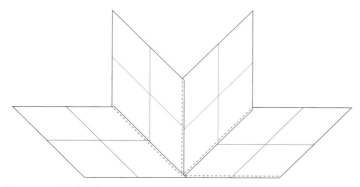

FIGURE 2–21. Half star.

SEWING DIRECTIONS

1 **MAKE STRING-PIECED DIAMONDS:** Sew strings crosswise on the paper foundations and trim them even with the edges of the paper.

2 **MAKE 8-POINTED STAR:** Join 2 diamonds to make a unit (Figure 2–18). Make 16 units. Stitch 2 units together to form a large diamond (Figure 2–19). Make 8 of these units.

Leave the seam allowances unsewn at the beginning and end of the seams for the next two steps.

Stitch 2 large diamonds together to form a quarter star (Figure 2–20). Press seam allowances as shown. Make 4 of these. Join 2 quarter star units to form a half star (Figure 2–21). Press seam allowances in the same direction as before. Make 2 half-star units.

Join the half-star units to complete the star. Notice that the seam allowances, all pressed in the same direction, form a swirl on the back of the star at the center (Figure 2–22).

3 **ADD BACKGROUND TRIANGLES AND SQUARES:** Notice that the star points are about ½" from the edges of the quilt, so that the star appears to float in the background. Cut the 24" square in quarters diagonally to make the 4 side triangles (Figure 2–23).

To make it easier to match seam lines for the set-in corner squares and side triangles, mark the seam intersections, on one corner of one (Figure 2–24). With right sides together, pin the short side of a side triangle to one side of a diamond. Be careful to match the seam between the diamonds with the ¼" mark on the triangle. The triangle will extend beyond the edge of the diamond at the outside edge.

Begin stitching at the ¼" mark and sew to the outside edge (Figure 2–25). Then pin the second side of the triangle in place and sew as before. Sew the remaining three triangles in the same manner. Press the seam allowances toward the triangles. Use the same technique to add the

STRING QUILTS WITH STYLE – Bobbie Aug & Sharon Newman

LONE STAR

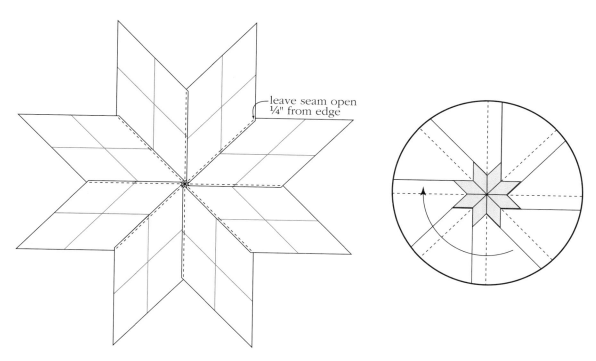

Figure 2–22. Press seam allowances in swirl at center.

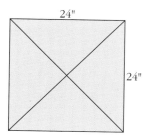

Figure 2–23. Cut square in quarters diagonally.

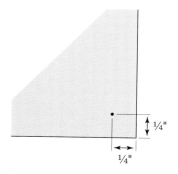

Figure 2–24. Mark seam intersections for set-in corner squares and side triangles.

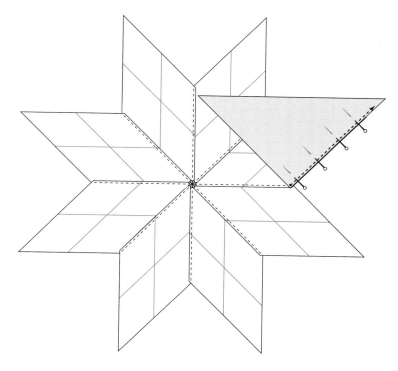

Figure 2–25. Pin triangle to diamond. Sew toward outside edge.

LONE STAR

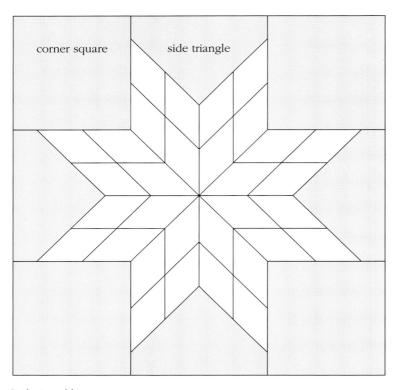

corner square side triangle

Quilt Assembly

Quilting Design

four corner squares to the star.

Trim the edges of the quilt top, leaving ¾" beyond the star tips all around. Be careful to keep the corners of the quilt square as you trim. Remove the paper foundations.

4 MARK QUILTING DESIGN: A variety of simple motifs, such as squares, circles, butterflies, and hearts, are quilted at random in the string-pieced diamonds. The background areas are quilted with concentric half or quarter circles.

5 FINISH QUILT: Layer the quilt top, batting, and backing, and baste the layers together. After quilting the design, remove the basting and trim the batting and backing even with the quilt top. Finish the edges with 2"-wide bias binding. Remember to sign and date your quilt.

SECTION THREE

Finishing Your Quilt

FINISHING YOUR QUILT

FIGURE 3–1. CROSS STRIPS, RIGHT SIDES TOGETHER

FIGURE 3–2. STITCH diagonally.

FIGURE 3–3. TRIM off EXTRA fabric.

FIGURE 3–4. PRESS SEAM ALLOWANCES OPEN.

FIGURE 3–5. BASTE THE bor-der INSERT TO THE QUILT INSIDE THE SEAM ALLOWANCE.

FIGURE 3–6. OVERLAP THE INSERTS AT THE CORNER.

ADDING BORDER INSERTS

This decorative treatment consists of flat, folded strips of fabric, similar to piping but without the cording inside. They are usually added before the borders are sewn to the quilt. To make an insert, cut strips along the straight of grain. Most are narrow, with only about ¼" showing on the face of the quilt. For a ¼" insert, you will need to cut strips 1" wide. To determine the length of each strip, measure the corresponding edge of the quilt top and add at least 1" for insurance.

If necessary, piece the strips to obtain the needed length for the border inserts, as follows: Position the ends of the strips with right sides together, at right angles to one another (Figure 3–1). Stitch diagonally at a 45° angle (Figure 3–2). Trim off the extra fabric, leaving ¼" seam allowances (Figure 3–3). Open the strips and press the seam allowances open (Figure 3–4). Fold the strip in half lengthwise, wrong sides together, and press.

To attach the border inserts, pin a folded strip to one side of the quilt, with raw edges aligned. Baste, stitching just inside the ¼" seam allowances (Figure 3–5). Cut the insert to the same length as the quilt edge. Repeat on the opposite side, then at the top and bottom edges of the quilt top, over-lapping the inserts at the corners (Figure 3–6). When you add the borders, you will catch the border inserts in the seams. Keep the insert fold toward the center of the quilt as you press the borders outward.

ADDING BORDERS

Borders that lie flat with smooth corners are easy to achieve, as long as you do some measuring. After the blocks have been sewn together, fold the bottom edge of the quilt up to the top edge to see if they are the same measurement. Similarly, fold the quilt in half lengthwise to see if the sides are the same length. Minor differences can be eased in sewing, but if you have a difference of ½" or more, you can make small adjustments in the seam allowances before add-ing your borders.

Measure the width and length of the quilt across the center. Cut the borders to these measurements, adding a couple of extra inches for insurance. It's easy to cut the extra off but you will hate adding a piece if you've underestimated!

MATCH THE BORDERS TO THE QUILT by marking the half and quarter measurements along the edge as follows: Begin by folding the quilt top to find the center of each side. Mark the center with a pin in each edge. To find the quarter mark, fold an edge of the quilt to meet the center pins. Mark the new fold with pins. Repeat for each quarter of the quilt (Figure 3–7). For a large quilt, you may want to fold the quilt again to mark the eighths. Measure the distance between two pins. Then, using the measurement from the quilt top, place pins along the border strips. Starting at the center marks, use the pins to match the borders to the quilt top.

FOR BUTTED CORNERS, pin the side border strips to the quilt top first, matching the corresponding pin marks. Sew the borders on with a ¼" seam allowance. Trim off any extra length even with the quilt edges. Press the seam allowances toward the borders. Repeat for the top and bottom.

FOR MITERED CORNERS, first mark the intersection of the seams, ¼" in from both edges, at the corners of the quilt (Figure 3–8). Find the half and quarter marks (and eighths if needed) on the quilt top and border strips. Match the strips to the quilt top, as with the butted borders. Sew all four borders to the quilt, starting and stopping at the seam intersections (Figure 3–9). Backstitch to anchor the seam lines at the intersections. At each corner, the two seams should just meet but not cross. Press the seam allowances toward the borders.

To complete the miter, fold the quilt in half diagonally, wrong side out, and match the raw edges of the borders and the border seams. Push the seam allowances out of the way so you can see the seam intersection. Use a ruler marked with a 45° angle to draw a line from the seam intersection to the border's edge. Pin along the drawn line and open the corner to see that any strong design elements, such as stripes, are matching. Re-align if necessary. Begin sewing at the intersection with a backstitch. Sew to the edge of the border (Figure 3–10). Trim the excess border length, leaving a ¼" seam allowance and press the allowance open (Figure 3–11). Trim off the points as shown.

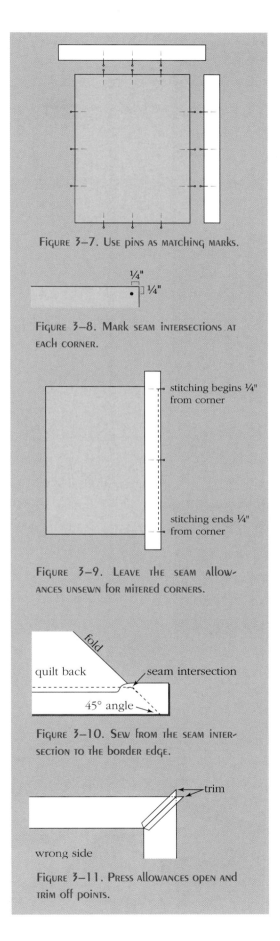

FIGURE 3–7. USE PINS AS MATCHING MARKS.

FIGURE 3–8. MARK SEAM INTERSECTIONS AT EACH CORNER.

stitching begins ¼" from corner

stitching ends ¼" from corner

FIGURE 3–9. LEAVE THE SEAM ALLOWANCES UNSEWN FOR MITERED CORNERS.

fold

quilt back

seam intersection

45° angle

FIGURE 3–10. SEW FROM THE SEAM INTERSECTION TO THE BORDER EDGE.

trim

wrong side

FIGURE 3–11. PRESS ALLOWANCES OPEN AND TRIM OFF POINTS.

Quilting designs add interest to the plain back- ground areas.

MARKING QUILTING DESIGNS

The graphic characteristics and overall beauty of string-pieced quilts come from the placement of fabrics and do not depend heavily on the quilting designs. However, quilting can enhance a string-pieced quilt. Quilting designs add interest to the plain background areas to balance the more exciting pieced blocks, and curved quilting lines can soften an angular patchwork of strings. The quilting pattern you choose may depend on whether you are hand or machine quilting. Hand quilting adds beauty, texture, and tradition, but, with the multitude of seams, machine quilting may be easier to do.

Where to put quilting stitches depends on the pattern and set of the quilt. For instance, you can quilt in the ditch, following the seam lines to outline basic design elements or color changes, or you can quilt individual patches to empha- size them. Patches can be quilted, without marking them, by sewing ¼" inside the seam lines by eye. Suggested quilting patterns accompany each of the quilts in this book. You may prefer to adapt the given design or to purchase and use sten- cils or patterns.

For decorative quilting, either on plain or patchwork areas, mark the designs on the quilt top so you have guide- lines to follow. It's generally easier to mark the top before it is layered with the batting and backing.

Prepare the quilt top for marking by pressing the entire top. (It is important that the quilt top be ironed before it is marked, because you could permanently heat-set the mark- ing ink.) Always test the markers you plan to use to make sure they can be removed. Chalk markers that brush off can be used for simple grids and straight lines. Mark a block at a time because the chalk rubs off as you handle the quilt. White and silver pencils should be kept sharp and used with a light touch. A scrap of cotton batting will help to remove these marks. Water-soluble markers require getting the quilt wet to remove any marks, so be sure you have prewashed all the materials.

CHOOSING BATTING

The batting choice depends on whether you will be hand or machine quilting your string-pieced quilt. Use a quality bat- ting and read the manufacturer's instructions. Be certain the batting purchased is at least 4" wider and longer than your quilt top.

Quilts with natural fiber batting (cotton, wool, or silk) have a good "hand," meaning they are soft and drape well. Batting that is 100% cotton needs to be quilted more heavily to prevent lumps, sometimes as closely as every ½" to 1". With a batting made of a cotton and polyester blend, the quilting lines can be as far apart as 3".

Bonded or glazed polyester batting needs only a moderate amount of quilting. In polyester batting, the lighter weights give a flatter look, medium weights are slightly puffier, while extra-heavy batts provide the loft of a contemporary comforter.

ADDING BACKING

Select a backing to enhance your quilt top. The colors in the quilt will usually determine the color of the quilting thread, which in turn may influence the choice of a backing fabric. A print fabric backing can be used by a novice quilter to help camouflage any irregularities in the quilting stitches.

It's best to cut and prepare the backing after the quilt top has been completed so that you can size it accurately. Adding 4" to both the width and length will give you room to maneuver when layering the quilt. For a large quilt, panels of fabric can be sewn together to make a backing. Cut away the selvages on all backing pieces because they can cause a seam to pucker. To avoid having a seam in the center of the quilt back, cut two lengths of fabric. Cut one piece in half lengthwise and join the halves to either side of the full-width piece.

The backing can also be pieced. Strive to make the design complement the quilt top in some way. More and more quiltmakers are sewing pieced backings on their quilts, as much for the creative opportunities as for the economic advantages.

LAYERING THE QUILT

For ease in quilting, press open any seam allowances on the backing. Check the batting package. Some cotton-blend batts require soaking, and some polyester batts should be tumbled in a cool dryer with a damp washcloth to relax the fold lines.

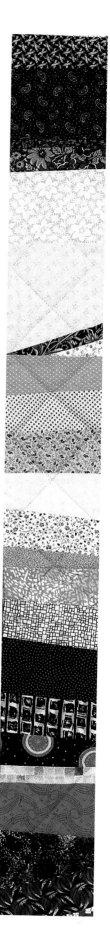

SELECT A
backing to
ENHANCE
YOUR quilt
TOP.

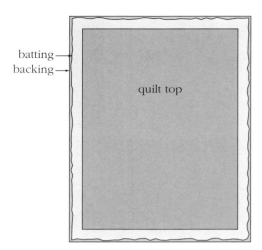

FIGURE 3–12. LAYER THE QUILT TOP, BAT-TING, AND BACKING.

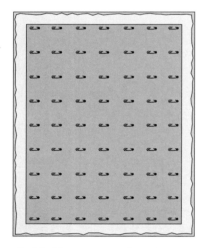

FIGURE 3–13. YOU CAN USE SAFETY PINS TO SECURE THE LAYERS.

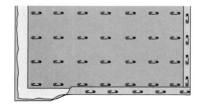

FIGURE 3–14. FOLD EXTRA BATTING AND BACKING OVER RAW EDGES AND PIN.

Place the backing, wrong side up, on a large table or clean carpet. Tape or pin to keep the backing flat and smooth but not stretched. Spread the batting over the backing and trim the batting to the same size as the backing.

Center the quilt top, right side up, on the batting and backing (Figure 3–12). Starting at the center of the quilt, pin all three layers together with 1" nickel-plated safety pins. Working out from the center, pin about every 4" (Figure 3–13).

Remove the tape or edge pins. Fold the backing over the batting and pin to protect the edges (Figure 3–14).

Begin quilting in the center of the quilt and work outward toward the edges.

SIGNING YOUR QUILT

Signing a quilt can be as simple as writing your name with a permanent-ink fabric pen, or it can be as elaborate as cross-stitching a label and embellishing it with embroidery. Some quiltmakers stitch their name and the date in the quilting design.

Include your name as the quiltmaker. Add your maiden name (it will be forgotten otherwise), the date the quilt was finished, and the city and state where you live. Use the label to tell the story of the quilt: What is the pattern? Was it made as a gift? Give as much information as possible.

If you choose to use a fabric pen, you can iron freezer paper (wax side toward the wrong side of the fabric) to the label to stabilize it. Practice writing slowly. Be sure to remove the paper before stitching the label to the back of the quilt.

Press under a ¼" seam allowance on the top and one side of the label. Position the label on a lower corner of the quilt back so that the two raw edges of the label will be encased in the binding. This not only saves sewing, but it provides extra insurance that the label will remain in place. Hand stitch the two folded edges to the quilt backing.

ATTACHING A SLEEVE

A sleeve is a tube of fabric, a casing through which a rod or slat can be inserted for hanging your quilt on a wall. If possible, prepare and sew a sleeve at the same time the quilt is made. Using a piece of the backing fabric will make the sleeve unobtrusive, but any fabric can be used. You can save some time and effort by sewing the sleeve on before attaching the binding.

To make a sleeve, cut or piece a 9"-wide strip that is the width of the quilt minus 2". Turn under each end ¼" twice, and stitch to hem (Figure 3–15). Fold the fabric in half lengthwise with wrong sides together. Center the sleeve on the back of the quilt, aligning raw edges (Figure 3–16). When the binding is added, the sleeve seam will be secured. Using a blind stitch, hand sew the bottom folded edge of the sleeve through the backing and batting only. Do not sew through to the quilt top.

If your quilt is finished, with its edges already bound, you can still add a sleeve for hanging. After the hemmed sleeve has been folded lengthwise, sew the raw edges together with a ¼" seam allowance, forming a tube. Press the tube so that the seam allowance is on the back of it. Center the sleeve on the back of the quilt along the top edge, just below the binding. Using a blind stitch, hand sew the top and bottom of the sleeve to the quilt through the backing and batting only (Figure 3–17).

MAKING BIAS BINDING

For a smooth, durable finish, cut binding strips on the bias, fold the strips in half lengthwise, and bind your quilt with this doubled strip. To obtain a long, continuous bias strip for binding, many quilters use a speed-cutting technique that starts with a square of fabric.

Cut a square of fabric the required size in half diagonally (Figure 3–18, page 90). Place the two resulting triangles together as shown (Figure 3–19), with right sides facing and edges even. Stitch by machine, leaving a ¼"-wide seam allowance. Press the allowances open.

You can use the grid on a rotary cutting mat for guide lines. Place the piece, wrong side down, with the bias edges parallel to the long lines of the mat (Figure 3–20).

Fold the upper tip down to meet the seam line (Figure 3–21), and fold the lower tip up to meet the seam line so the straight-of-grain edges meet on the diagonal. Make sure the edges do not overlap. This diagonal is the butting line. Secure with pins.

Keep the bias edges even on the left side and as even as

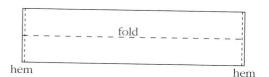

FIGURE 3–15. Hem both ends of sleeve.

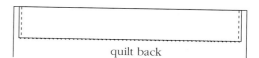

FIGURE 3–16. Raw sleeve edge will be caught in binding.

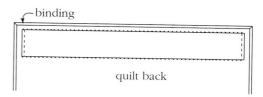

FIGURE 3–17. Hand sew sleeve to quilt.

SIGNING A QUILT CAN BE AS SIMPLE AS WRITING YOUR NAME.

Making Bias Binding

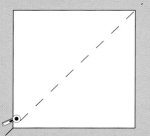

Figure 3–18. Cut fabric square diagonally.

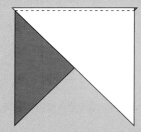

Figure 3–19. Sew the triangles together.

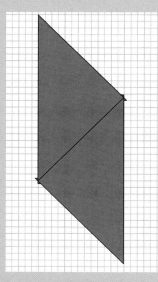

Figure 3–20. Place the piece on a rotary cutting mat.

butting line

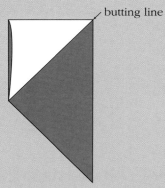

Figure 3–21. Fold tips to meet butting line.

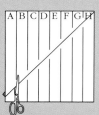

discard

Figure 3–22. Discard too-narrow last strip.

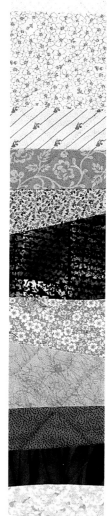

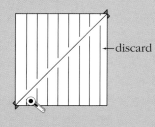

Figure 3–23. Complete cuts for strips A and H (top fabric only).

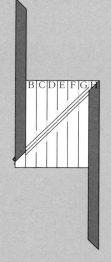

Figure 3–24. Draw ¼" seam lines on each side of the butting line. Finger crease guide lines across the butting line.

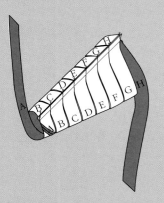

Figure 3–25. Shift the bottom edge to the right one strip width.

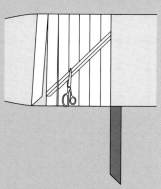

Figure 3–26. Finish the cuts across the seam.

String Quilts with Style – Bobbie Aug & Sharon Newman

possible on the right. (If you are left-handed, reverse these directions.) Begin cutting the binding to the desired width from the left. Stop cutting about 1" before the butting line and start again 1" after it. The cut should not cross the butting line. Continue to cut across the fabric in parallel lines, interrupting each cut at the butting line. Discard the last strip, which is too narrow (Figure 3–22).

Refer to Figure 3–23. Lift up the end of strip A and use scissors to complete the cut at the butting line. Repeat for the last strip (H). To help you realign the strips in the next step, draw ¼" seam lines on both ends at the butting line, as shown in Figure 3–24. Then mark where each cut will cross the seam lines you have just drawn. This is easily done by finger creasing a fold from each cut to the butting line.

Re-align the fabric edges at the butting line by moving the bottom strips to the right one strip (Figure 3–25). Pin the re-aligned edges, right sides together, using the folds and drawn seam lines as guides. (The seam will look odd at this point, and it will not lie flat.) Stitch on the drawn seam line to form a tube, leaving a ¼"-wide seam allowance.

Slide the fabric tube onto an ironing board, seam roll, or tightly rolled towels to press the seam allowances open. Using scissors, cut across the previously uncut portions of fabric (Figure 3–26). You will end up with a long, continuous strip. For doubled binding, fold the strip in half lengthwise with wrong sides together and press.

ATTACHING BINDING. Starting a few inches from a corner, align the raw edges of the binding with the raw edge of the quilt top. (Be sure to leave about 8" of the beginning end of the strip unsewn so you can finish the ends later.) Stitch the binding to the quilt, using a seam allowance equal to the desired width of binding that will be visible on top of the quilt. When you come to a corner, stop stitching at the seam line for the next side of the quilt (Figure 3–27). Backstitch to secure the seam at that point.

Fold the binding to the back of the quilt and finger crease the binding at the fold (Figure 3–28). Fold the binding up at a 45° angle at the corner (Figure 3–29). Fold the binding down and align the creased fold with the top edge of the quilt and the raw binding edge with the raw quilt top edge (Figure 3–30). Begin sewing again where the previous stitching stopped; backstitch to secure (Figure 3–31).

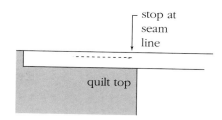

FIGURE 3–27. STOP STITCHING AT SEAM LINE AND BACKSTITCH.

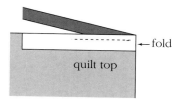

FIGURE 3–28. FINGER CREASE BINDING AT fold.

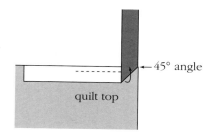

FIGURE 3–29. Fold binding up at 45° ANGLE.

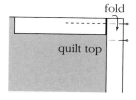

FIGURE 3–30. Fold binding back down.

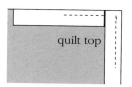

FIGURE 3–31. BEGIN SEWING AGAIN AT SEAM LINE.

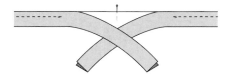

FIGURE 3–32. MARK CENTER WITH A PIN.

FIGURE 3–33. PIN THE ENDS TOGETHER AT THE PIN.

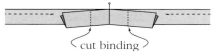

cut binding

FIGURE 3–34. TRIM OFF THE ENDS.

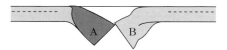

A   B

FIGURE 3–35. UNFOLD THE ENDS.

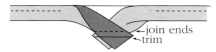

join ends
trim

FIGURE 3–36. JOIN THE ENDS AND TRIM.

FIGURE 3–37. FINISH SEWING BINDING TO QUILT.

quilt back

FIGURE 3–38. AT CORNER, SEW RIGHT SIDE OF BINDING FIRST.

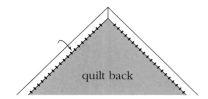

quilt back

FIGURE 3–39. THEN SEW LEFT SIDE TO COMPLETE MITER.

Continue sewing the binding strip to the quilt edges, repeating the mitering steps at each corner. Stop stitching about 8" from the point where you began sewing the binding to the quilt.

JOINING BINDING ENDS. Insert a straight pin in the middle of the space between where the stitching begins and ends (Figure 3–32).

Smooth the binding in place and pin the strips to each other, but not to the quilt, at the point where the center pin is inserted in the quilt (Figure 3–33). Remove the first pin.

Measuring from the remaining pin, trim off the ends of the strips, leaving a tail on each end that is the width of the folded binding (Figure 3–34). For example, if the folded binding strip is 1" wide, trim each end 1" beyond the pin.

To join the strips at a 45° angle, remove the pin and open the left strip so that it is wrong side up (Figure 3–35, end A) and open the right strip right side up (end B). Place end A on top of end B at right angles, right sides together. Stitch diagonally across the ends, from inside corner to inside corner (Figure 3–36). Trim off excess fabric, leaving ¼" seam allowances.

Finger press the seam allowances open. Refold the strip as before. Finish sewing the binding to the quilt (Figure 3–37).

SEWING BINDING IN BACK. Fold the binding over the raw edges of the quilt. Using thread to match the binding, blind stitch the binding to the back of the quilt. Be careful not to let the stitches come through to the front. At the corners, sew the right side of the binding first (Figure 3–38), then sew the left side to create a mitered corner (Figure 3–39).

Gallery

Quilts & Quilt Tops

GALLERY

YELLOW SPIDERWEB, 66" x 80", 1936, by Elvera Traweek, Wilson, Texas. Made for her, and put into her hope chest.

GALLERY

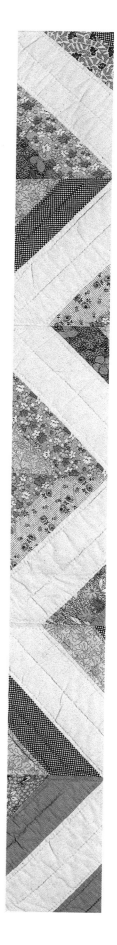

ALL OVER DIAMONDS, 58" x 84", CIRCA 1950. From the collection of Onita Steinhauser of Wilson, Texas. Purchased in the Old Mill Trade Days in Post, Texas.

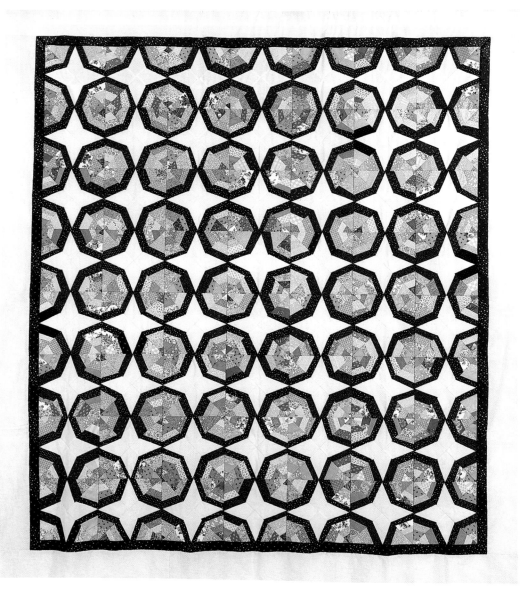

BLUE SPIDERWEB, top, 98" x 109", 1996, by LaVerne Stolle, Slaton, Texas. "I would quilt this, but I keep finding one I want to quilt first."

GALLERY

LONE STAR, ⊤oᴘ, 72" x 72", 1998, by **Loʀᴇɴᴀ Rɪɴᴇʏ, Slᴀᴛoɴ, Tᴇxᴀs.** Lorena said she was "using up all the little leftover strips from several quilts that she has given away."

GALLERY

RED AND BLACK SPIDERWEB, тор, 70" x 90". The red and
black fabrics used to set together the string pieces of 1950s fabrics
give a unity to the whole.

GALLERY

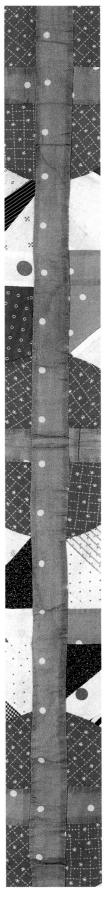

SNOWBALL, top, 72" x 76". The fabrics in this string-pieced top are from the last decade of the nineteenth century. The Nile green listed in the 1897 Sears catalog is displayed in the setting strips. Note the many different polka dots. From the collection of Sharon Newman.

GALLERY

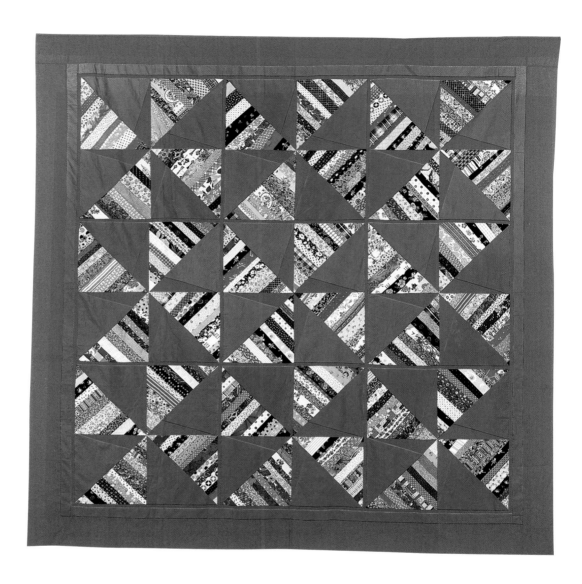

DOUBLE PINWHEEL, top, 100" x 100", 1994, by Dorothy Perry, Lubbock, Texas. Dorothy used scraps from the 1960s to create a king-size quilt top.

GALLERY

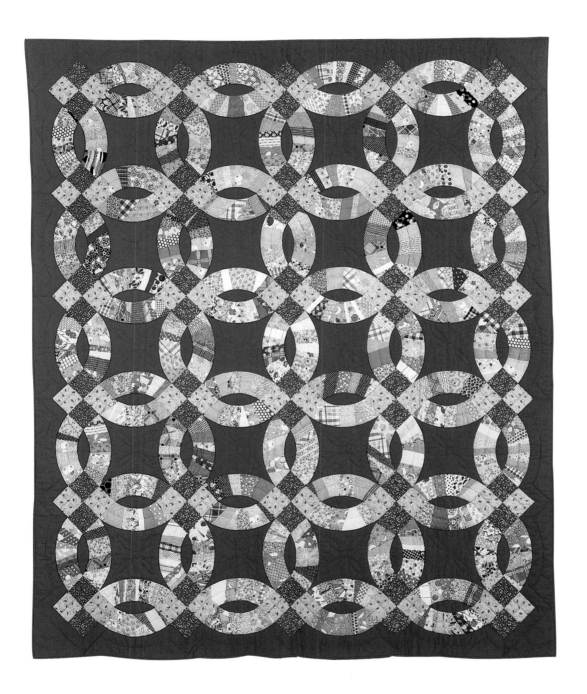

DOUBLE WEDDING RING, 70" x 82". Bands pieced on 1928
catalog pages by Bessie Sawyer Newman. Quilt completed in 1993
by Sharon Newman.

INDIAN HATCHET, 68" x 87", ᴄɪʀᴄᴀ 1930. This quilt was col-
lected in Indiana by Mary Ann Wheatly. The design is one often
string pieced — just use the same color diagonally across the center.

ABOUT THE AUTHORS

Bobbie Aug and Sharon Newman met in Paducah, Kentucky, at the 1989 American Quilter's Society Show. Both were in the first group tested and certified as quilt appraisers by AQS. Currently, both serve as members of the AQS Appraiser Certification Program Committee. Sharon also serves as the program's administrator. Both learned to sew on treadle sewing machines, Bobbie in Illinois and Sharon in Indiana. Their love and appreciation of quilts brought them together, and they have been friends ever since. Together, the two have traveled to quilt shows, presented programs, judged quilt shows, taught classes, and appraised quilts.

Sharon's interest in quiltmaking began in Indiana as the granddaughter of a prolific quiltmaker. Since marrying her husband, Tom, and rearing three daughters, Tracy, Vicki, and Carol, Sharon has focused on quilts and quiltmaking with a well-known business, The Quilt Shop, and participation in the Texas Quilt Search. She has written seven books on quiltmaking and quilt history, and she is nationally recognized for her reproduction fabric lines from Moda Fabrics.

Bobbie Aug was inspired by the quiet, dignified beauty of nineteenth-century quilts and began making quilts 30 years ago. She became a quilt dealer, quilt collector, quilt shop owner, and quilt show consultant and producer, focusing on anything related to quilts and quiltmaking. Bobbie lives in Colorado Springs, Colorado, with her husband, Norm. Their family includes son Tony, daughter Carrie, Brittany spaniels Angel and Sadie, and a nasty cat named Phannie.

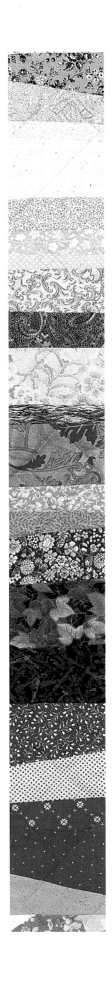

AQS Books on Quilts

This is only a partial listing of the books available from the American Quilter's Society. AQS books are known worldwide for timely topics, clear writing, beautiful color photos, and accurate illustrations and patterns. The following books are available from your local bookseller, quilt shop, or public library. If you are unable to locate certain titles in your area, you may order by mail from the AMERICAN QUILTER'S SOCIETY, P.O. Box 3290, Paducah, KY 42002-3290. Add $2.00 for postage for the first book ordered and 40¢ for each additional book. Include item number, title, and price when ordering. Allow 14 to 21 days for delivery. Customers with Visa, MasterCard, or Discover may phone in orders from 7:00–5:00 CST, Mon.–Fri., 1-800-626-5420.